2nd Workshop on Sentiment Analysis and Linguistic Linked Data (SALLD-2)

Held at LREC 2022

Marseille, France
20 – 25 June 2022

Editors:

Ilan Kernerman
Sara Carvalho
Carlos A. Iglesias
Rachele Sprugnoli

ISBN: 978-1-7138-6136-2

Printed from e-media with permission by:

Curran Associates, Inc.
57 Morehouse Lane
Red Hook, NY 12571

proceedings.com

Some format issues inherent in the e-media version may also appear in this print version.

Association for Computational Linguistics
209 N. Eighth Street
Stroudsburg, Pennsylvania 18360

Phone: 1-570-476-8006
Fax: 1-570-476-0860

acl@aclweb.org

Additional copies of this publication are available from:

Curran Associates, Inc.
57 Morehouse Lane
Red Hook, NY 12571 USA
Phone: 845-758-0400
Fax: 845-758-2633
Email: curran@proceedings.com
Web: www.proceedings.com

LREC 2022 Workshop
Language Resources and Evaluation Conference
20-25 June 2022

2nd Workshop on Sentiment Analysis and Linguistic Linked Data (SALLD-2)

PROCEEDINGS

Editors:
Ilan Kernerman
Sara Carvalho
Carlos A. Iglesias
Rachele Sprugnoli

Proceedings of the LREC 2022 workshop on Sentiment Analysis and Linguistic Linked Data (SALLD-2)

Edited by:
Ilan Kernerman, Sara Carvalho, Carlos A. Iglesias, Rachele Sprugnoli

For more information:
European Language Resources Association (ELRA)
9 rue des Cordelières
75013, Paris
France
http://www.elra.info
Email: lrec@elda.org

Proceedings of the *2nd Workshop on Sentiment Analysis and Linguistic Linked Data*

Preface

The Linguistic Linked Open Data (LLOD) initiative was created within the Open Linguistics Working Group (OLWG) of the Open Knowledge Foundation to foster the publication of language resources in open licenses. The SALLD (Sentiment Analysis and Linguistic Linked Data) workshop aims at contributing to the LLOD initiative by providing a discussion forum about the usage of Linguistic Linked Data principles in the Sentiment Analysis field, to explore relevant principles, methodologies, resources, tools, and applications, and understand the primary approaches, their advantages, limitations, and available resources and case studies. SALLD-2 is the second edition of the workshop and is held in conjunction with LREC 2022 in Marseille, France, on June 24, 2022. It follows SALLD-1, which was co-located with LDK 2021 – 3rd Conference on Language, Data and Knowledge – in Zaragoza, Spain, on September 1, 2021. The SALLD series was initiated in the framework of the NexusLinguarum COST Action – European network for Web-centred linguistic data science (CA 18209) and has its support.

We are delighted to have a keynote talk, entitled *From Data to Meaning in Representation of Emotions*, from an invited speaker, Dr. Anna Fensel, Associate Professor at Wageningen University and Research, in the Netherlands, and at University of Innsbruck, Austria. Her current research includes emotion analysis based on knowledge graphs.

The workshop accepted five papers. Three papers are related to sentiment lexicons; one is related to the harmonization of language resources, and another to the exploitation of information available in the Linked Open Data cloud for sentiment analysis.

In the first category, the paper *Movie Rating Prediction using Sentiment Features* by Apóstolo et al. provides a new sentiment lexicon, Expanded OntoSenticNet (EON), which combines OntoSenticNet with SentiWordNet. This new language resource is used to predict movie ratings. In the same way, the paper *Sentiment Analysis of Serbian Old Novels* by Stanković et al. publishes a polarity lexicon in Serbian based on three existing lexicons (NRC, Affin, and Bing), the ontolex-lemon model and the sentiment vocabulary Marl. Finally, the paper *Evaluating a New Danish Sentiment Resource: the Danish Sentiment Lexicon, DSL* by Schneidermann and Pedersen provides an evaluation of Danish sentiment lexicons. We want to highlight the importance of publishing sentiment non-English lexicons for resource-scarce languages.

The second category has been addressed by the paper *O-Dang! The Ontology of Dangerous Speech Messages* by Stranisci et al., which defines an interoperable knowledge graph to link linguistic resources related to dangerous speech. This knowledge graph has been populated with eight language resources in Italian on dangerous speech, which shows the considerable potential of linked data technology to interlink language resources.

Finally, the use of open linked data for sentiment analysis is exploited by the paper *Correlating Facts and Social Media Trends on Environmental Quantities Leveraging Commonsense Reasoning and Human Sentiments* by McNamee et al. This paper analyzed how external information (e.g., temperature or pollution) can be combined with the insights of sentiment analysis.

Ilan Kernerman
Sara Carvalho
Carlos A. Iglesias
Rachele Sprugnoli

Organizers

Ilan Kernerman - K Dictionaries - Lexicala
Sara Carvalho - Universidade de Aveiro
Carlos A. Iglesias - Universidad Politécnica de Madrid
Rachele Sprugnoli - Università degli Studi di Parma

Program Committee

Valerio Basile, University of Turin (ITALY)
Paul Buitelaar, NUI Galway (IRELAND)
Davide Buscaldi, Université Paris 13 Sorbonne (FRANCE)
Erik Cambria, Nanyang Technological University (SINGAPORE)
Sara Carvalho, Universidade de Aveiro (PORTUGAL)
Hugo Gonçalo Oliveira, University of Coimbra (PORTUGAL)
Carlos A. Iglesias, Universidad Politécnica de Madrid (SPAIN)
Ilan Kernerman, K Dictionaries – Lexicala (ISRAEL)
Barbara Lewandowska-Tomaszczyk, State University of Applied Sciences, Konin (POLAND)
Chaya Liebeskind, Jerusalem College of Technology (ISRAEL)
Francesco Mambrini, Università Cattolica del Sacro Cuore (ITALY)
Kiemute Oyibo, University of Waterloo (CANADA)
Marco Carlo Passarotti, Università Cattolica del Sacro Cuore (ITALY)
Marco Respocher, University of Verona (ITALY)
Rachele Sprugnoli, Università degli Studi di Parma (ITALY)
Dimitar Trajanov, ss. Cyril and Methodius University, Skopje (NORTH MACEDONIA)
Slavko Žitnik, University of Ljubljana (SLOVENIA)
Arkaitz Zubiaga, Queen Mary University of London (UNITED KINGDOM)

Acknowledgement

Special thanks to Ana Todorovska, from the Faculty of Computer Science and Engineering, Ss Cyril and Methodius University, Skopje, for managing the SALLD website https://salld.org/.

Table of Contents

Workshop Program

Friday, June 24, 2022

14:00–14:05 ***Welcome***

14:05–15:00 *Invited talk: From Data to Meaning in Representation of Emotions*
Anna Fensel

15:00–15:30 *O-Dang! The Ontology of Dangerous Speech Messages*
Marco Antonio Stranisci, Simona Frenda, Mirko Lai, Oscar Araque, Alessandra Teresa Cignarella, Valerio Basile, Cristina Bosco and Viviana Patti

15:30–16:00 *Movie Rating Prediction using Sentiment Features*
João Ramos, Diogo Apóstolo and Hugo Gonçalo Oliveira

16:00–16:30 ***Break***

16:30–17:00 *Evaluating a New Danish Sentiment Resource: the Danish Sentiment Lexicon, DSL*
Nina Schneidermann and Bolette Pedersen

17:00–17:30 *Correlating Facts and Social Media Trends on Environmental Quantities Leveraging Commonsense Reasoning and Human Sentiments*
Brad McNamee, Aparna Varde and Simon Razniewski

17:30–18:00 *Sentiment Analysis of Serbian Old Novels*
Ranka Stanković, Miloš Košprdić, Milica Ikonić Nešić and Tijana Radović

18:00–18:15 ***Closure***

Proceedings of the SALLD-2 Workshop @LREC2020, page 1
Language Resources and Evaluation Conference (LREC 2022), Marseille, 24 June 2022

From data to meaning in representation of emotions

Anna Fensel

Wageningen Data Competence Center and Consumption and Healthy Lifestyles Chair Group, Wageningen University and Research, 6708 PB Wageningen, The Netherlands

University of Innsbruck, Department of Computer Science, Technikerstr. 21a, A-6020 Innsbruck, Austria

anna.fensel@wur.nl

Historically, now we have an unprecedentedly large amount of data available in various systems, and the growth of data volumes is rapid and continuous. The numbers of scientific papers published per year are higher than ever before. While it is desirable to have the context of the users of a social system known and represented in a machine-readable form, capturing this context is notoriously complex (as social context is more difficult to measure with simple sensors, unlike some physical characteristics). This complexity applies especially to the domain of emotions, but also to other context information relevant for social systems and social sciences (for example, in case of experimental study set up in sociology or marketing, detailed user profiles, exact background and experimental settings need to be recorded in a precise manner). Which data and scientific findings get shared, for which purposes, and how? How to address open and closed data, and reproducibility crisis? How to convert Big Data into Smart Data, which is interpretable by both machine and human? And how to make sure that the resulting Smart Data is trustworthy and appropriately handling biases? In my talk, I discuss these questions from the technical perspective, and give examples for relevant solutions implemented with Semantic Web technology, linked data, knowledge graphs and FAIR (Findable, Accessible, Interoperable, Reusable) data management. Specifically, I will be discussing experiences with combining machine learning and knowledge graphs for semantic representation of emotions. Further, I will talk about research data infrastructures and tools for social sciences that can facilitate semantic interoperability and bring more meaning with sharing semantic representation of context, such as one about emotions. Such semantic representations and infrastructures can serve as a basis for industrial applications, including recommender systems, personal assistants and chatbots, and also serve to improve research data management in social sciences.

Proceedings of the SALLD-2 Workshop @LREC2020, pages 2–8
Language Resources and Evaluation Conference (LREC 2022), Marseille, 24 June 2022

O-Dang! The Ontology of Dangerous Speech Messages

Marco A. Stranisci*, Simona Frenda*◇, Mirko Lai*, Oscar Araque⋆, Alessandra T. Cignarella*, Valerio Basile*, Viviana Patti*, Cristina Bosco*

* Department of Computer Science - University of Turin, Turin, Italy
◇ PRHLT Research Center - Universitat Politècnica de València, Valencia, Spain
⋆ Intelligent Systems Group - ETSI Telecomunicación - Universidad Politécnica de Madrid, Madrid, Spain
{marcoantonio.stranisci simona.frenda, mirko.lai, alessandrateresa.cignarella, valerio.basile, viviana.patti, cristina.bosco}@unito.it
o.araque@upm.es

Abstract

Inside the NLP community there is a considerable amount of language resources created, annotated and released every day with the aim of studying specific linguistic phenomena. Despite a variety of attempts in order to organize such resources has been carried on, a lack of systematic methods and of possible interoperability between resources are still present. Furthermore, when storing linguistic information, still nowadays, the most common practice is the concept of "gold standard", which is in contrast with recent trends in NLP that aim at stressing the importance of different *subjectivities* and points of view when training machine learning and deep learning methods. In this paper we present O-Dang!: The Ontology of Dangerous Speech Messages, a systematic and interoperable Knowledge Graph (KG) for the collection of linguistic annotated data. O-Dang! is designed to gather and organize Italian datasets into a structured KG, according to the principles shared within the Linguistic Linked Open Data community. The ontology has also been designed to account a *perspectivist* approach, since it provides a model for encoding both gold standard and single-annotator labels in the KG. The paper is structured as follows. In Section 1. the motivations of our work are outlined. Section 2. describes the O-Dang! Ontology, that provides a common semantic model for the integration of datasets in the KG. The Ontology Population stage with information about corpora, users, and annotations is presented in Section 3.. Finally, in Section 4. an analysis of offensiveness across corpora is provided as a first case study for the resource.

Keywords: Knowledge Graph, LLOD, Hate Speech, Misogyny, Irony, Sarcasm, NLP, Annotations, Subjectivity, Perspectivism.

1. Introduction and Motivation

In this day and age, in almost every research field – as well as in Computational Linguistics – it is considered an enormous wealth to have the presence of manually annotated data sets in order to implement Machine Learning and Deep Learning pipelines. In the last 15 years there has been a very extensive effort within many research groups that deal with Natural Language Processing (NLP) for the creation, development and maintenance of corpora of linguistic data annotated with regard to various phenomena.

Nowadays, there are thousands of data sets that model similar phenomena in many different languages, and it often happens that each research group models a phenomenon on the basis of their own annotation scheme, usually not shared with other researchers, who are involved in studying similar phenomena on different languages. Another frequent case in the modeling of linguistic phenomena is to develop new annotations adding further layers of information on top of pre-existing ones to train, for instance, models based on multitask learning.

The research idea we would like to present in this paper stems from the need to provide a more structured organization to the myriad of linguistic resources and datasets developed in the NLP field, and to guarantee interoperability and dialogue between similar resources.

Among the many projects that already devoted their efforts in creating a bridge between sentiment and emotion analysis and linguistic data, we mostly referred to EUROSENTIMENT (Sánchez Rada et al., 2014) developing a common language resource representation model based on established Linked Data formats such as Onyx (Sánchez-Rada and Iglesias, 2016) and Marl (Westerki and Sánchez-Rada, 2013).

In this paper, we describe the creation of a Linguistic Linked Open Data (LLOD) resource, focused on collecting dangerous messages that indirectly contribute to the spread of discriminatory contents, thus called **The Ontology of Dangerous Speech** (O-Dang!).

Dangerous Speech has been defined by Benesch (2012) as a speech that "has a reasonable *chance* of catalyzing or amplifying violence by one group against another, given the circumstances in which it was made or disseminated". This *chance* materializes when the circumstances in which the speech takes place consist of: 1) a powerful speaker or source with a high degree of influence, 2) an audience that believe to be subject to a threat, 3) a social and historical context propitious for the violence, 4) the means of dissemination (such as social media), 5) the content of the speech that aims at the process of dehumanization, guilt attribution, threat construction, destruction of alternatives, creation of a new semantics of the violence conceived as admirable, linked to praiseworthy qualities and based on specific biased references that justify it (Leader Maynard and Benesch, 2016). Dangerous speech, therefore, is a type of speech that aims at contributing to create a climate of violence and intolerance against protected groups of people, such as women, immigrants, religious minorities, and others.

As some scholars highlighted, there are various rhetorical and pragmatic devices that play a part in the expression of dangerous utterances. For instance, Grimminger and Klinger (2021) and Frenda et al. (2019) reflected on the use

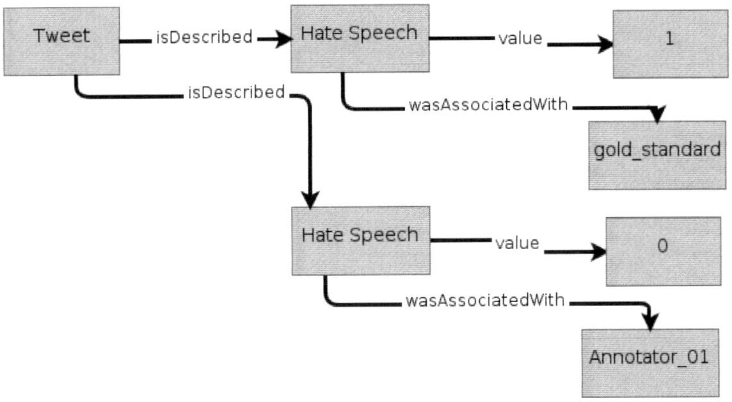

Figure 1: A snapshot of the O-Dang Semantic Model in which gold standard and un-aggregated annotations are encoded.

of offensive and toxic communication in tweets expressing a stance towards specific political candidates (such as Biden and Trump) or sensible social issues involving a particular target such as women (like feminist movements or abortion). Others focused more on the use of the ironic language to lessen the negative tones of the hateful messages, making their automatic recognition challenging (Nobata et al., 2016; Frenda et al., 2022). The employment of these kinds of devices actually lets speakers or users to be less explicit in their claims, limiting, thus, their exposure.

From this perspective, we designed an ontology for storing existing Italian corpora in a Knowledge Graph (KG) that is interoperable and that takes into account general characteristics of the various NLP datasets annotated for various dimensions of hate such as Hate Speech (HS), misogyny, stereotypes, and offensive and aggressive language. The semantic model is general enough to populate the KG with other corpora focused on orthogonal phenomena to hate, such as stance or ironic language, realizing a tool that is open to collaborative effort of the scientific community.

In this sense we are inspired by the work of Bender and Friedman (2018) in which the authors propose data statements as a design solution and professional practice for natural language processing technologists to be followed when creating a linguistic resource and making it available to other researchers.

Furthermore, our work follows the directives of the *Perspectivist Data Manifesto*[1] (Basile, 2020), and that is, we do not limit ourselves to consider the data of written texts and the gold standard labels, but – where possible – we try to store in the KG the labels of the different annotations in un-aggregated form for emphasizing the importance of the different perspectives and points of view of individual subjectivities of human annotators. Finally, our work is also inspired by Lewandowska-Tomaszczyk et al. (2021) which is focused on aligning several phenomena correlated to discrimination in a unique semantic model.

The contributions to be found in this article are the following:

- **The O-Dang! Ontology**[2], a semantic model aimed at describing and linking a variety of datasets containing Dangerous Speech and orthogonal phenomena;
- A KG containing 11 existing Italian NLP data sets on Dangerous Speech and parallel phenomena. The KG serves as a first case study for providing interoperability between corpora annotatet fo Dangerous Speech;
- **an Entity Linking pipeline** for recovering the specific targets of Dangerous Speech and abusive language;
- **un-aggregated annotations** of the datasets developed by our research group in the past years;

The resulting KG will be available through endpoint SPARQL, allowing several applications, among which:

- exporting personalized portion of the KG for the study of specific phenomena across corpora and the configuration of different training sets.
- querying all Dangerous Speech referred to specific persons and groups
- filtering gold standard and un-aggregated annotation
- querying the communication interaction among users and messages

2. The O-Dang! Ontology

The O-Dang! Ontology provides a general encoding for the harmonization of different datasets in a unique resource. The model relies on existing authoritative resources, such as Dolce (Gangemi et al., 2002), Prov-O (Lebo et al., 2013), and FRBR (Tillett, 2005)[5], and represents three aspects

[1] https://pdai.info/.

[2] https://github.com/marcostranisci/o-dang

[3] Implicit or explicit.

[4] Analogy, euphemism, context shift, false assertion, hyperbole, oxymoron-paradox, rhetorical question, other.

[5] Prefixes of existing ontologies reused in our model are the following: Dolce (dul), Prov-O (prov), FRBR (frbr). Properties of classes of O-Dang! are introduced by ':'

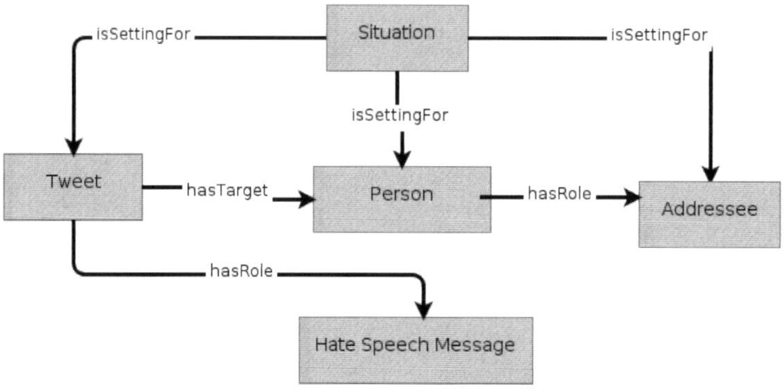

Figure 2: A portion of the O-Dang Semantic Model where a communicative situation with a participant is represented.

about data: (i) the encoding of the annotated text, (ii) the provenance of annotations, (iii) the conversational situation in which the annotated message is present.
A message is encoded as a FRBR:EXPRESSION embedded in one or more FRBR:MANIFESTATION and linked to one or more annotated corpora through the property **dul:isPartOf**. All annotation schemes are represented as subclasses of DUL:DESCRIPTION, since each scheme may be intended as a shared description of a concept between researchers and annotators. As it can be observed in Figure 1, a DUL:ISDESCRIBED as 'Hate Speech' with a specific value. Such a modeling enables the comparison of different schemes adopted for annotating same concepts (Poletto et al., 2021) (eg: binary, scalar). Finally, the **prov:wasAssociatedWith** property links all annotations to their annotators Figure 1 shows two types of annotator: gold_standard, namely a label to identify all aggregated annotations, and a set of individual annotators for researchers interested in querying un-aggregated data from the KG. It is important to notice that no socio-demographic information about annotators is provided within O-Dang!, but only anonymized ids of the type 'annotator_*n*'.
Messages annotated as expressing a given concept are also encoded within a conversational situation, that is a **dul:Situation** in which people, messages, and groups may hold a role. Such representation is focused on the interaction between messages, concept related to Dangerous Speech, and Agents, allowing to query all messages that express a given phenomenon, and have a specific category as a target. In Figure 2 the representation of an HS message may be observed. The Situation DUL:ISSETTINGFOR a Tweet with the role of Hate Speech Message, which is the result of the annotation process depicted in 1. The target of this message has also setting in the same situation with the role of Addressee. Below, an example of materialized triples encoding a HS message against Cécile Kyenge[6] is provided.

```
odang_situation_1342 a :Situation;
    isSettingFor :@ckyenge;
    :isSettingFor [
    a :Tweet;
    :hasRole HateSpeechMessage;
    :hasText ''@ckyenge per fare
    sentire     a casa voi africani
    e musulmani e stranieri'';
    :hasTarget :@ckyenge
    ];
    @ckyenge a :Person;
    :hasRole :Addressee;
    :gender :female;
    :citizenship :ITA;
    :placeOfBirth :Kambove.
```

[6]She is an Italian politician and ex member of the European Parliament.

3. Datasets and Ontology Population

The O-Dang! KG includes $898,016$ triples about $62,193$ tweets and $21,972$ users. The Ontology Population stage was performed in two steps: the integration of different data sets in the KG, and a Entity Linking pipeline for the population of the ontology with socio-demographic information about users who are target of Dangerous Speech.

3.1. Dataset Integration

Table 1 shows the datasets that are already populating O-Dang!. As said in Section 1., these corpora are related to Dangerous Speech and parallel phenomena such as irony and stance. For each dataset, we provide the bibliographic reference, textual genres of data, the considered phenomena and the values used to label their presence, and finally the type of annotation ('aggregated' and 'un-aggregated') provided by authors. The un-aggregated annotations reveal the different perspectives or subjectivities on the perception of Dangerous Speech, as well as the difficulty of annotation of the phenomenon and, consequently, of ambiguous cases. For instance, the following news headline (Example 1) was annotated by `annotator_1` as hateful and by `annotator_2` as non-hateful.

(1) *Alessandria, straniero con ascia e martello aggredisce coppia in casa*
→Alexandria, a foreigner with ax and hammer attacks a couple at home

Beyond the clearness of the guidelines, the interpretation of

name	reference	genre	phenomena	annotation	size
IronITA 2018	(Cignarella et al., 2018)	tweets	irony (0/1), sarcasm (0/1), — for some data: type of irony[3] category of irony[4] PoS tags & UD	un-aggregated	4,849
AMI 2018	(Fersini et al., 2018)	tweets	misogyny (0/1), category (stereotype / dominance derailing / sexual harassment discredit), target classification (active/passive)	aggregated	5,000
HaSpeeDe 2018	(Sanguinetti et al., 2018)	facebook posts and tweets	hate speech (0/1)	aggregated	7,996
Hate Speech Corpus	(Sanguinetti et al., 2018)	tweets	hate speech (0/1), stereotype (0/1), aggressiveness (0/1), irony (0/1), intensity (0–>4)	un-aggregated	6,928
SardiStance 2020	(Cignarella et al., 2020)	tweets	stance (against/favor/none) irony (0/1)	un-aggregated	3,242
AMI 2020	(Fersini et al., 2020)	tweets	misogyny (0/1) aggressiveness (0/1)	aggregated	7,000
HaSpeeDe 2020	(Sanguinetti et al., 2020)	tweets and news headlines	hate speech (0/1), stereotype (0/1), aggressiveness (0/1), irony (0/1), sarcasm (0/1) — for some data: offensiveness (0/1), intensity (0–>4) nominal utterances	un-aggregated	8,602
Moral ConvITA	(Stranisci et al., 2021)	tweets	moral stance	un-aggregated	1,722
Populismo Penale	N/A	tweets	stance (against/favor/none)	un-aggregated	12,479
Silvia Romano Corpus	N/A	tweets	stance, abusive language	un-aggregated	4,913
Crowd-HS	N/A	tweets	hate speech (0-7)	un-aggregated	926

Table 1: Summary of the datasets which are already populating O-Dang!

the instances is subjective and relies on the backgrounds of the annotators (Akhtar et al., 2021).

3.2. Entity Linking pipeline

Information about addressees of dangerous messages from Twitter is provided in the KG through an Entity Linking pipeline. Names of each user who is mentioned in a reply have been retrieved through the Twitter API and then searched using Google KG. After a disambiguation process relying on exact string matching between the name provided in input and Google KG output, and on the Google KG score, all the corresponding Wikidata ID were retrieved. Finally, sociodemographic information about each user has been collected from Wikidata. The resulting number of users mapped within the KG is 344. For each, the following information are provided: date of birth, place of birth, country of citizenship, sex or gender, occupation, political party. Below, an example of user associated with such properties is shown.

```
odang_usr_7986 a :Person;
    :hasID 322933929;
    :gender female;
    :birthYear 1985;
    :countryOfCitizenship :ITA;
    :placeOfBirth :Lugano;
    :occupation :politician;
    :politicalParty :DemocraticParty .
```

4. Lexical Analysis

To perform lexical analysis catching the offensiveness of the messages contained in the datasets that at the moment populate O-Dang!, we employed HurtLex (Bassignana et al., 2018). HurtLex is a multilingual lexicon of hateful words created from the Italian lexicon "Le Parole per Ferire" by Tullio de Mauro. The entries in the lexicon are categorized in 17 types of offenses (see Table 2) enclosed in two macro-categories: *conservative* (words with literally offensive sense) and *inclusive* (words with not literally offensive sense, but that could be used with negative connotation). In particular, we considered only the conservative version of the hurtful categories which have been mapped within O-Dang! through OntoLex-Lemon (McCrae et al., 2017). Each *conservative* word in HurtLex is represented as the following:

```
:IT1241 a :LexicalEntry;
rdfs:label 'fannullone'/'loafer';
lexinfo:partOfSpeech :Noun;
:isDescribed :dmc.
:dmc a :Offensive;
rdfs:label 'moral defects' .
```

The idea is to exploit HurtLex as a means to cross-evaluate the offensiveness of the datasets in the KG (even those which are not annotated expressly as dangerous), and to provide a further description of them.

category	**length**	**description**
PS	254	Ethnic Slurs
RCI	36	Location and Demonyms
PA	167	Profession and Occupation
DDP	496	Physical Disabilities and Diversity
DDF	80	Cognitive Disabilities and Diversity
DMC	657	Moral Behavior and Defect
IS	161	Words Related to Social and Economic advantages
OR	144	Words Related to Plants
AN	775	Words Related to Animals
ASM	303	Words Related to Male Genitalia
ASF	191	Words Related to Female Genitalia
PR	138	Words Related to Prostitution
OM	145	Words Related to Homosexuality
QAS	536	Descriptive Words with Potential Negative Connotations
CDS	2042	Derogatory Words
RE	391	Felonies and Words Related to Crime and Immoral Behavior
SVP	424	Words Related to the Seven Deadly Sins of the Christian Tradition

Table 2: HurtLex Categories.

In this way, we have characterized the datasets with HurtLex using a straightforward approach. For each document, the words that are included in each HurtLex category and in the document are counted. This outputs a count for each HurtLex category that is related to a document. To aggregate these counts on a dataset, we average over all documents.

Table 3 shows the result of the described lexical analysis. Such characterization profiles the use of selected HurtLex categories across all datasets. One of the most interesting categories in these datasets, due to its prevalence, is CDS (derogatory words). It can be seen that it is specially relevant in the hate speech and stance datasets.

Continuing with this, the one of the highest metric for the CDS category is obtained in the HaSpeeDe 2018 dataset. Interestingly enough, when looking at this same metric aggregated by annotation class, we see a shift. The HaSeeDe 2018 describes a hate speech binary annotation. For the negative class, the CDS metric has a value of 0.1165 while for the positive class it reaches 0.1546. This observation gives further insight into the language of the data.

5. Conclusion and Future Work

In this paper, we presented O-Dang!, a KG of Italian data sets annotated for Dangerous Speech-related phenomena. The KG includes $62,193$ tweets and $258,704$ annotations both aggregated and un-aggregated. The underlying Semantic Model enables to perform comparative analysis between data sets and phenomena. A first exploratory analysis of offensiveness across corpora has also been provided.

Future work will be devoted to employ this resource to fully inform the systems of abusive language detection, gathering useful pragmatic, semantic and interactional patterns. Moreover, O-Dang! will be integrated with corpora containing different genres of texts in various languages. Finally, a more robust Entity Linking pipeline will be applied, in order to provide more information about Dangerous Speech targets, that may be used for building more explainable systems for abusive language detection.

6. Acknowledgements

The work of M. A. Stranisci was funded by the project "Be Positive!" (under the 2019 "Google.org Impact Challenge on Safety" call). The work of S. Frenda, V. Patti and C. Bosco was supported by the European project "STERHEOTYPES - STudying European Racial Hoaxes and sterEOTYPES" funded by the Compagnia di San Paolo and VolksWagen Stiftung under the "Challenges for Europe" call for Project (CUP: B99C20000640007). The work of A. T. Cignarella and V. Basile was supported by the project "Toxic Language Understanding in Online Communication - BREAKhateDOWN" funded by Compagnia di San Paolo (ex-post 2020). The work of Oscar Araque has been funded by the European Union's Horizon 2020 project Participation (grant agreement no. 962547) and the help of the "Programa Propio" from "Universidad Politécnica de Madrid".

7. Bibliographical References

Akhtar, S., Basile, V., and Patti, V. (2021). Whose opinions matter? Perspective-aware models to identify opinions of hate speech victims in abusive language detection. *CoRR*, abs/2106.15896.

Basile, V. (2020). It's the end of the gold standard as we know it. On the impact of pre-aggregation on the evaluation of highly subjective tasks. In Giuseppe Vizzari, et al., editors, *Proceedings of the AIxIA 2020 Discussion Papers Workshop co-located with the 19th International Conference of the Italian Association for Artificial Intelligence (AIxIA2020), Anywhere, November 27th, 2020*, volume 2776 of *CEUR Workshop Proceedings*, pages 31–40. CEUR-WS.

Bender, E. M. and Friedman, B. (2018). Data statements for natural language processing: Toward mitigating system bias and enabling better science. *Transactions of the Association for Computational Linguistics*, 6:587–604.

Dataset	PS	DDP	DDF	DMC	ASM	ASF	QAS	CDS	SVP
IronITA 2018	0.0080	0.0217	0.0031	0.0431	0.0151	0.0103	0.0210	0.0693	0.0054
HaSpeeDe 2018	0.0228	0.0430	0.0015	0.0540	0.0313	0.0180	0.0350	0.1286	0.0088
Hate Speech Corpus	0.0172	0.0345	0.0013	0.0453	0.0240	0.0141	0.0282	0.1068	0.0079
SardiStance 2020	**0.0275**	0.0584	0.0050	**0.0617**	0.0413	0.0333	0.0333	0.1275	0.0110
HaSpeeDe 2020	0.0199	0.0396	0.0016	0.0548	0.0263	0.0149	0.0307	0.1128	0.0074
Moral ConvITA	0.0175	0.0420	0.0014	0.0467	0.0236	0.0175	0.0331	0.1176	0.0080
Populismo Penale	0.0142	0.0454	0.0015	0.0402	0.0156	0.0260	0.0226	**0.1478**	0.0064
Silvia Romano Corpus	0.0196	**0.0589**	0.0036	0.0429	**0.0429**	**0.0339**	**0.0405**	0.1024	**0.0107**
Crowd-HS	0.0151	0.0356	0.0011	0.0508	0.0140	0.0130	0.0313	0.1274	0.0097

Table 3: Characterization of the O-Dang! datasets using HurtLex.

Benesch, S. (2012). Dangerous speech: A proposal to prevent group violence. *Voices That Poison: Dangerous Speech Project proposal paper.*

Frenda, S., Noriko, K., Patti, V., Rosso, P., et al. (2019). Stance or insults? In *Proceedings of the Ninth International Workshop on Evaluating Information Access (EVIA 2019), a Satellite Workshop of the NTCIR-14 Conference*, pages 15–22. National Institute of Informatics.

Frenda, S., Cignarella, A. T., Basile, V., Bosco, C., Patti, V., and Rosso, P. (2022). The unbearable hurtfulness of sarcasm. *Expert Systems with Applications*, 193.

Gangemi, A., Guarino, N., Masolo, C., Oltramari, A., and Schneider, L. (2002). Sweetening ontologies with DOLCE. In *International Conference on Knowledge Engineering and Knowledge Management*, pages 166–181. Springer.

Grimminger, L. and Klinger, R. (2021). Hate towards the political opponent: A Twitter corpus study of the 2020 US elections on the basis of offensive speech and stance detection. In *Proceedings of the Eleventh Workshop on Computational Approaches to Subjectivity, Sentiment and Social Media Analysis*, pages 171–180, Online, April. Association for Computational Linguistics.

Leader Maynard, J. and Benesch, S. (2016). Dangerous speech and dangerous ideology: An integrated model for monitoring and prevention. *Genocide Studies and Prevention: An International Journal*, 9(3).

Lebo, T., Sahoo, S., McGuinness, D., Belhajjame, K., Cheney, J., Corsar, D., Garijo, D., Soiland-Reyes, S., Zednik, S., and Zhao, J. (2013). Prov-o: The prov ontology.

Lewandowska-Tomaszczyk, B., Žitnik, S., Bączkowska, A., Liebeskind, C., Mitrović, J., and Valunaite Oleskeviciene, G. (2021). LOD-connected offensive language ontology and tagset enrichment. In *Proceedings of the Workshops and Tutorials held at LDK 2021 co-located with the 3rd Language, Data and Knowledge Conference (LDK 2021)*, pages 135–150. CEUR-WS.

McCrae, J. P., Bosque-Gil, J., Gracia, J., Buitelaar, P., and Cimiano, P. (2017). The ontolex-lemon model: development and applications. In *Proceedings of eLex 2017 conference*, pages 19–21.

Nobata, C., Tetreault, J., Thomas, A., Mehdad, Y., and Chang, Y. (2016). Abusive language detection in online user content. In Jacqueline Bourdeau, et al., editors, *Proceedings of the 25th International Conference on World Wide Web, WWW 2016, Montreal, Canada, April 11 - 15, 2016*, pages 145–153. ACM.

Poletto, F., Basile, V., Sanguinetti, M., Bosco, C., and Patti, V. (2021). Resources and benchmark corpora for hate speech detection: a systematic review. *Language Resources and Evaluation*, 55(2):477–523.

Sánchez Rada, J. F., Vulcu, G., Iglesias Fernandez, C. A., and Buitelaar, P. (2014). EUROSENTIMENT: Linked data sentiment analysis. In *Proceedings of the ISWC 2014 Posters & Demonstrations Track a track within the 13th International Semantic Web Conference (ISWC 2014)*, pages 145–148. CEUR-WS.

Tillett, B. (2005). What is FRBR? A conceptual model for the bibliographic universe. *The Australian Library Journal*, 54(1):24–30.

8. Language Resource References

Bassignana, E., Basile, V., and Patti, V. (2018). Hurtlex: A multilingual lexicon of words to hurt. In *5th Italian Conference on Computational Linguistics, CLiC-it 2018*, volume 2253, pages 1–6. CEUR-WS.

Cignarella, A. T., Frenda, S., Basile, V., Bosco, C., Patti, V., and Rosso, P. (2018). Overview of the EVALITA 2018 Task on Irony Detection in Italian Tweets (IronITA). In *Proceedings of the 7th Evaluation Campaign of Natural Language Processing and Speech Tools for Italian (EVALITA 2018)*. CEUR-WS.org.

Cignarella, A. T., Lai, M., Bosco, C., Patti, V., and Rosso, P. (2020). SardiStance @ EVALITA2020: Overview of the Stance Detection in Italian Tweets. In *Proceedings of the 7th Evaluation Campaign of Natural Language Processing and Speech Tools for Italian (EVALITA 2020)*. CEUR-WS.org.

Fersini, E., Nozza, D., and Rosso, P. (2018). Overview of the EVALITA 2018 task on automatic misogyny identification (AMI). In Tommaso Caselli, et al., editors, *Proceedings of the Sixth Evaluation Campaign of Natural Language Processing and Speech Tools for Italian. Final Workshop (EVALITA 2018) co-located with the Fifth Italian Conference on Computational Linguistics (CLiC-it 2018), Turin, Italy, December 12-13, 2018*, volume 2263 of *CEUR Workshop Proceedings*. CEUR-WS.

Fersini, E., Nozza, D., and Rosso, P. (2020). AMI @ EVALITA2020: Automatic misogyny identification. In Valerio Basile, et al., editors, *Proceedings of the Seventh Evaluation Campaign of Natural Language Processing and Speech Tools for Italian. Final Workshop (EVALITA*

2020), Online event, December 17th, 2020, volume 2765 of *CEUR Workshop Proceedings*. CEUR-WS.

Sánchez-Rada, J. F. and Iglesias, C. A. (2016). Onyx: A linked data approach to emotion representation. *Information Processing & Management*, 52(1):99–114.

Sanguinetti, M., Poletto, F., Bosco, C., Patti, V., and Stranisci, M. (2018). An Italian Twitter corpus of hate speech against immigrants. In *Proceedings of the Eleventh International Conference on Language Resources and Evaluation (LREC 2018)*, Miyazaki, Japan, May. European Language Resources Association (ELRA).

Sanguinetti, M., Comandini, G., Di Nuovo, E., Frenda, S., Stranisci, M. A., Bosco, C., Tommaso, C., Patti, V., and Irene, R. (2020). HaSpeeDe 2 @ EVALITA2020: Overview of the EVALITA 2020 Hate Speech Detection Task. In *EVALITA 2020 Seventh Evaluation Campaign of Natural Language Processing and Speech Tools for Italian*, pages 1–9. CEUR.

Stranisci, M., De Leonardis, M., Bosco, C., and Patti, V. (2021). The expression of moral values in the twitter debate: a corpus of conversations. *IJCoL. Italian Journal of Computational Linguistics*, 7(7-1, 2):113–132.

Westerki, A. and Sánchez-Rada, J. F. (2013). Marl ontology specification. V1.0, May.

Proceedings of the SALLD-2 Workshop @LREC2020, pages 9–18
Language Resources and Evaluation Conference (LREC 2022), Marseille, 24 June 2022

Movie rating prediction using sentiment features

João Ramos, Diogo Apóstolo, Hugo Gonçalo Oliveira
CISUC, DEI, Universidade de Coimbra, Portugal
uc2017254040@student.uc.pt, japostolo@student.dei.uc.pt, hroliv@dei.uc.pt

Abstract

We analyze the impact of using sentiment features in the prediction of movie review scores. The effort included the creation of a new lexicon, Expanded OntoSenticNet (EON), by merging OntoSenticNet and SentiWordNet, and experiments were made on the "IMDB movie review" dataset, with the three main approaches for sentiment analysis: lexicon-based, supervised machine learning and hybrids of the previous. Hybrid approaches performed the best, demonstrating the potential of merging knowledge bases and machine learning, but supervised approaches based on review embeddings were not far.

Keywords: Motive Rating Prediction, Sentiment Analysis, Supervised Machine Learning, Linked Data

1. Introduction

Sentiment Analysis (SA) has been applied to determine the sentiment conveyed by people in various situations. For instance, it can be useful for recommender systems, which may exploit the sentiment expressed by an user for items they have consumed, predict their sentiment for other items, and recommend those for which a positive sentiment is predicted. One particular application centres on the use of the sentiment conveyed by the words, as features for predicting the scores of movies or product reviews (Schuller and Knaup, 2010; Kapukaranov and Nakov, 2015; Agarwal et al., 2015; Cernian et al., 2015). Another popular application is sentiment analysis in social media publications (Rosenthal et al., 2017; Jovanoski et al., 2015).

Most of the previous adopt a very specific pipeline, presented in Figure 1. They start by either choosing a pre-existing dataset or creating one. The dataset is then preprocessed to be more easily analysed with sentiment extraction methods, often based on a sentiment lexicon, supervised machine-learning, or a hybrid of both. In some literature (Kapukaranov and Nakov, 2015; Schuller and Knaup, 2010), sentiment analysis is not the final goal, and the predicted sentiment is used as the input for another task. This is the case of our work, where sentiment is used for predicting movie review scores.

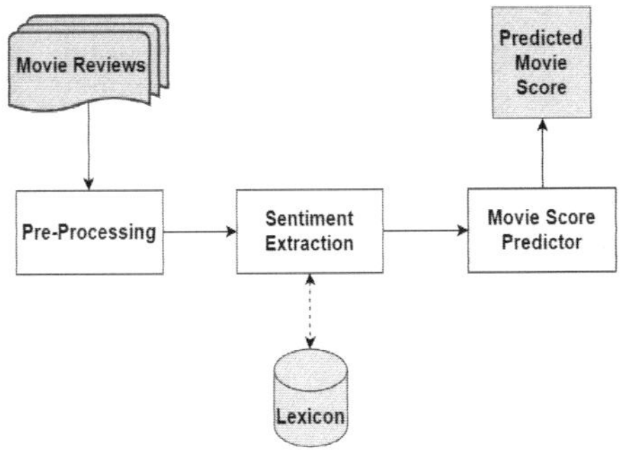

Figure 1: Typical pipeline

In order to better understand the impact of exploiting sentiment features for our goal, we experiment with the three different approaches: lexicon-based, supervised machine learning (SML) and hybrids of the previous. Our main contributions are:

- The creation of a new lexicon, Expanded OntoSenticNet (EON), which combines information from two sentiment resources, SenticNet (Cambria et al., 2010) and SentiWordNet (Esuli and Sebastiani, 2006);
- Experimentation with the recent IMDB movie review dataset (Pal et al., 2020);
- Attempting to predict the score of a review, not just the polarity, as most approaches do;
- Confirmation that sentiment features are useful for the prediction of review scores.

This paper is organized as follows: Section 2 overviews datasets and approaches for sentiment analysis; Section 3 describes the dataset and lexicons used in this work; Section 4 is on the setup of the experiments conducted, including details on implementation and parameterization; Section 5 reports and discusses the outcomes of the experiments; Section 6 concludes with the main take-aways and future work.

2. Background and Related Work

In this section, the details of the pipeline in Figure 1 is further elaborated upon, starting with a brief overview of the typical datasets used, followed by an explanation of each step.

2.1. Datasets

IMDB movie review datasets have been made available [1 2], with reviews and information like the publication date and name of the author. However, reviews

[1] https://www.kaggle.com/mantri7/imdb-movie-reviews-dataset/activity

[2] https://www.kaggle.com/lakshmi25npathi/imdb-dataset-of-50k-movie-reviews

are generally labelled as negative or positive, sometimes assuming a direct mapping between scores and polarity. We argue that, even if sentiment contributes to the score, they are different things. An exception is a dataset where reviews have a user-given score between 1 and 10 (Pal et al., 2020).
This kind of dataset can be collected from movie review websites like IMDB or Metacritic, which contain reviews in different languages (Schuller and Knaup, 2010; Kapukaranov and Nakov, 2015; Denecke, 2008). An alternative source of professional reviews is Rotten Tomatoes(Pang and Lee, 2005).
A similar methodology can and has been adopted for the creation of datasets for sentiment analysis in social networks (Jovanoski et al., 2015; Lobo and Pandya, 2019; Neethu and Rajasree, 2013).

2.2. Sentiment Extraction

Sentiment extraction refers to the application of natural language processing (NLP) for identifying and extracting subjective information in source materials. It is extensively applied to comments, posts and reviews, as a way of acquiring people's opinions about a subject (Shi et al., 2019). Sentiment extraction can be roughly separated into three main approaches: lexicon-based, supervised machine learning, and a hybrid.

2.2.1. Lexicon-Based Approaches

Semantic lexicons compile words and expressions together with sentiment-related information, such as the typical polarities they transmit. Lexicon-based approaches for sentiment classification resort to such resources for acquiring the polarity of words, which they combine towards sentence or document sentiment. The performance of these approaches is thus highly dictated by the quality of the lexicon, its size and how well it fits the specific problem. Lexicons are too resource-intensive to handcraft and, without the help of automatic methods, may fail to have a great coverage. To minimize this problem, one can start with a small dictionary of sentiment words and their polarity, and expand it iteratively through the analysis of: other available lexicons (Hu and Liu, 2004; Kim and Hovy, 2004); or corpora, e.g., based on co-occurrence statistics like PMI (Church and Hanks, 2002).
SentiWordNet (Esuli and Sebastiani, 2006), SenticNet (Cambria et al., 2010), GeneralInquirer (GI) (Stone et al., 2007), LIWC (Tausczik and Pennebaker, 2010) and VADER (Hutto and Gilbert, 2014) are among the most popular sentiment lexicons. SentiWordNet and SenticNet are known as valence-based, because they assign a continuous score for each word, not just a label (e.g., positive or negative). More specifically, in SentiWordNet each word has three scores: positivity, negativity and objectivity, and the sum of the three must add up to 1. SenticNet covers over 10,000 concepts, each with a score between -1 (negative) to 1 (positive). The VADER lexicon is based on LIWC, ANEW and GI, complemented by a list of western emoticons, sentiment related acronyms and slang. Though not considered by most of the other lexicons, these additions are a relevant for sentiment extraction. The new vocabulary was examined and given a score by multiple people. The VADER tool uses the VADER lexicon to calculate the polarity of sentences with four scores: negative, positive, neutral and compound.
Another lexicon (Agarwal et al., 2015) was built from SenticNet, SentiWordNet and GI. An ontology was created from ConceptNet (Speer et al., 2016) and other ontologies with domain-specific content. Towards sentiment extraction, document features are matched to the ontology, and their relevance is considered to be proportional to their distance to the root of the ontology. The final polarity of an opinion word is the result of $lexicon\ polarity \times height\ of\ ontology$. Results show that the use of a context-specific ontology provides better results overall.
After choosing a lexicon, the polarity of a sentence can be computed by aggregating the sentiment values of included concepts that also occur in a sentiment lexicon. The polarity of all the sentences in a document will contribute to the overall polarity of the document. For example, SentiWordNet has been used for assigning a positivity, negativity and objectivity score to each sentence, from which the overall score was computed with logistic regression (Denecke, 2008). Similar approaches using SentiWordNet were adopted in other works (Bhoir and Kolte, 2015; Cernian et al., 2015)
Another work (Schuller and Knaup, 2010) explored GI and WordNet (Miller et al., 1991) for sentiment extraction simultaneously with the target of the sentiment. Out of the resulting expressions, the relevant ones are selected with the help of ConceptNet, to finally compute the document polarity score.

2.2.2. Supervised Machine Learning Approaches

An alternative to lexicons, which are not always suitable or available, is supervised machine learning (SML). These, however, require annotated data, which, for sentiment extraction, means textual documents and their manually-assigned polarity.
Moreover, to be exploited by SML approaches, documents generally have to be represented as numeric vectors, which can be obtained with algorithms such as TF-IDF, Doc2Vec, or more recently, sentence transformers. These may, however, make the interpretation of the results harder, if possible.
Traditional text classification algorithms have been used for determining the polarity of the document, including SVM, Naive Bayes and kNN (Yasen and Tedmori, 2019; Baid et al., 2017a; Baid et al., 2017b). Some test a range of classifiers, and assess the results with measures like accuracy, precision, recall, F1 and AUC. When tested in movie reviews, Random Forests proved superior to the remaining classifiers (Yasen and Tedmori, 2019). In the same scenario, SML approaches were also compared with lexicon-based (Schuller and Knaup, 2010). SML used a bag of n-grams representa-

tion and relied on an SVM to determine the polarity of the text document.
Experiments were also conducted to predict the score given by the user in the review, again with bag of n-grams features and a regression algorithm (SVR). SML was superior to the lexicon approaches, both in F1 and accuracy, but both methods had much difficulty for classifying negative reviews.
With the Deep Learning boom, there was a push to explore deep neural networks for sentiment extraction. Similarly to some traditional approaches, these models take embedded documents as their input, but they are more adequate for the large number of inputs the embedding generates. Recurrent Neural Networks (RNN) (Tang et al., 2015) were used for generating word representations from word to sentence level and then from sentence to document level, and applied to sentiment analysis. This resulted in better accuracy than previous approaches in several datasets. Traditional word embeddings (Word2Vec, GloVe, FastText) were also explored as the input of a Convolutional Neural Network (CNN), achieving the best accuracy in comparison to other tested algorithms (Vizcarra et al., 2018). LSTM networks were experimented in this task, with improvements achieved by ATAE-LSTM (Wang et al., 2016), an attention-based LSTM, which extracts features from each sentence and analyses the sentiment polarity of each aspect. Yet, since 2018, as it happens for other NLP tasks, the trend is to fine-tune neural language models based on transformers. Here, BERT performs especially well for sentence sentiment analysis (Habimana et al., 2020).

2.2.3. Hybrid Approaches

In hybrid approaches, the sentiment of a document is extracted with the help of both lexicons and content features, such as the number of positive/negative/objective sentences (Kapukaranov and Nakov, 2015). Document or sentence embeddings may be further exploited (Kapukaranov and Nakov, 2015; Keerthi Kumar et al., 2018; Kim et al., 2019).
For example, dependency parsing was combined with machine learning (Poria et al., 2014). Dependency-based rules are used for better capturing the role of a concept within a sentence and, if concepts are found in SenticNet, their polarity is obtained from this resource. Otherwise, an Extreme Learning Machine classifier, trained on a movie review dataset, is used to guess the sentence polarity.
Also, for movie reviews, content features (e.g., words, bigrams, emoticons) were exploited together with aggregated positive and negative scores of words, according to an automatically-generated lexicon, also considering meta information about each movie (e.g., actors, genre, director) (Kapukaranov and Nakov, 2015). From them, experiments were conducted for predicting the rating of the review with a SVM classifier or regression (SVR or logistic regression). A similar approach was adopted in the domain of social media sentiment analysis (Jovanoski et al., 2015).
A different task is to predict the success of movies from their plot summaries (Kim et al., 2019), also considering their sentiment. More precisely, classification considers the sentiment score of a document, computed with the VADER lexicon for each sentence, and its representation by ELMo (Peters et al., 2018) embeddings.

2.3. Current Challenges

Some authors have confirmed that using a general purpose sentiment lexicon like General Inquirer, with no context specific information, leads to a poor performance (Schuller and Knaup, 2010). This can be minimized both by the creation of larger lexicons, e.g., by merging existing ones and adding domain-specific information. An alternative is to adopt machine learning, which may also exploit lexicon features. Here, the lack of context may also result in more false positives (Schuller and Knaup, 2010), so it is recommended that training data is on the application domain. Moreover, to further increase performance, a larger set of features can be exploited, including meta information about the domain (Kapukaranov and Nakov, 2015).
We should add that much work with movie reviews aims at classifying polarity, i.e., whether a review is positive or negative. Even if, sometimes, the ground truth is obtained by converting the rating directly (Pang et al., 2002; Maas et al., 2011), classifying the polarity is not exactly the same problem as predicting the rating. As such, it would be interesting to further research on actually predicting the rating, e.g., with a regression algorithm, as others have done (Kapukaranov and Nakov, 2015; Schuller and Knaup, 2010).

3. Data

This section is on the data used in our experimentation, namely the dataset and the lexicons.

3.1. Dataset

We used a subset of the "IMDB Movie Reviews Dataset" (Pal et al., 2020), which originally contained nearly 1 million movie reviews from 1,150 different movies, across 17 genres[3]. For each review, the following features are provided:

- **username:** which identifies the review's author;
- **rating:** a score in the 1–10 interval, given by the author to the movie;
- **helpful:** the number of people that found the review helpful;
- **total:** the number of people who classified the review either as helpful or unhelpful;
- **date:** the date the review was written in;
- **title:** the title of the review, usually a short sentence that summarizes the author's opinion;

[3]https://ieee-dataport.org/open-access/imdb-movie-reviews-dataset

- **review:** a text review describing the opinion of the author about the movie.

For illustrative purposes, Figure **??** shows two entries of the dataset.
Our goal was to predict the rating by exploiting features extracted from the review. It is important to note that the rating distribution is not balanced.
However, using the full dataset would be impractical for the available time and computational power. We thus worked on a random selection of 10,000 instances of the dataset, including about 7,500 reviews rated higher than 5 and 2,500 rated 5 or lower (see Figure 3). Afterwards, the dataset was split into a cross-validation and a held-out evaluation set. The former contained 90% of the instances and the latter contained the remaining 10%. The cross-validation set was used to tune the parameters of the SML algorithms, which were then tested in the evaluation set. Lexicon-based approaches, which do not require training, are evaluated on the evaluation set.

3.2. Lexicons

The lexicons explored in this work were SenticNet, more precisely, its ontology version, OntoSenticNet, and SentiWordNet. Having in mind the benefits of combining lexicons, we created a new ontology, Expanded OntosenticNet (EON), with information from both. From OntoSenticNet, we extracted the 'polarity' annotation, a score between -1 (negative) and 1 (positive) available for each word and expression. From SentiWordNet, we used the 'positive' (SWN_Pos) and 'negative' (SWN_Neg) scores, each ranging from 0 to 1. This way, each entry in the lexicon would have at most three sentiment-related scores.
OntoSenticNet is represented in RDF/OWL and was queried with RDFLib[4]. SentiWordNet scores were obtained with the NLTK[5] interface available for querying this resource.
In EON, words or expressions that are in only one of the lexicons stay only with the annotations from the lexicon they are in. SentiWordNet words with only objectivity scores were not considered, as they would only add noise to the predictions.
EON is available in RDF[6]. To look up the polarity scores, we use the SPARQL query in Listing 1. Table 1 illustrates the possible results, with examples for different tokens. The 'polarity' column comes from OntoSenticNet, and the other two come from SentiWordNet.

```
SELECT ?SenticConcept ?text ?polarity ?SWN_Positive
?SWN_Negative WHERE {
 ?SenticConcept :text ?text.
 ?SenticConcept :text <token> .
 ?SenticConcept :polarity ?polarity .
 ?SenticConcept :SWN_Positive ?SWN_Positive.
 ?SenticConcept :SWN_Negative ?SWN_Negative.
}
```

Listing 1: SPARQL query for retrieving polarities from EON

Table 1: Example results for SPARQL query in Listing 1, for different tokens.

Token	polarity	SWN_Pos	SWN_Neg
abhorrent	-0.44	0.00	0.75
good	0.66	0.69	0.00
food	0.03	0.00	0.04

4. Experimentation Setup

This section details the setup of the conducted experiments, namely on: data preprocessing, tested approaches, and parameterization of the algorithms, also covering the adopted evaluation metrics.

4.1. Preprocessing

The reviews were prepossessed with Python's NLTK package. This step included: the removal of HTML tags; sentence splitting; the removal of punctuation and stopwords; tokenization and lemmatization.

4.2. Experimented Approaches

Experimentation was performed with three different groups of approaches described here.

4.2.1. Lexicon Approach

In order to get the polarity of the reviews, EON is queried, with RDFLib, for each lemmatized token in the document. Whenever the token is in EON, the three polarity values (polarity, SWN_Pos, SWN_Neg) are obtained with the query in Listing 1. The token sentiment score s is calculated according to equation 1, where p is the polarity value in OntoSenticNet, and swp and swn are respectively SWN_Pos and SWN_Neg.

$$s = \frac{(p + \frac{(swp - swn)}{2})}{2} \tag{1}$$

Seven different options were tested for aggregating token sentiment values in a sentence sentiment, namely:

- **Mean:** mean value for all tokens;
- **Max:** highest token value (positive or negative);
- **Max 3/5:** mean of 3/5 highest token values;
- **Neg 2/3/4:** mean of all token values, but with negative values weighting twice/three times/four times as more as positive;

Since review scores range from 1 to 10, the result of the previous methods, which range from 0 to 1, was mapped to the 1–10 interval. Two different mapping

[4] https://rdflib.readthedocs.io/en/stable/
[5] https://www.nltk.org/
[6] https://github.com/DiogoApostolo/EON

username: red95king **rating:** 1 **helpful:** 3 **total:** 8 **date:** 10/01/2002
title: *The Moronic & Ridiculous*
review: *This move was so dumb I don't even know where to begin. Put next to this, films "Stone Cold", "Harley Davidson and the Marlboro Man", and "Road House" look like cinematic masterpieces. If only it were true that you could roll a car 12 times at 100 miles per hour and come out with hardly a scratch. Granted there are some outstanding stunts, but not enough action overall to offset the non-sense plot and 3rd rate acting. Don't get me wrong I consider Vin Diesel a pretty good actor, but the script sounds like it was written for (or perhaps by) 8 year olds. Vin, your talents were wasted buddy. Watch "Grand Prix" instead.*

username: Shervin1982 **rating:** 4 **helpful:** 0 **total:** 0 **date:** 16/05/2003
title: *Neo has to choose!*
review: *I wouldn't call it a movie, rather a sequence of actions. If you're looking forward to watching fight scenes for over an hour, this is a must see. But the movie as a whole, is very poor and aimless. Martix reloaded compare to its prequal is very disappointing.*

Figure 2: Reviews for movies "The Fast and the Furious" (2001) and "The Matrix Reloaded" (2003).

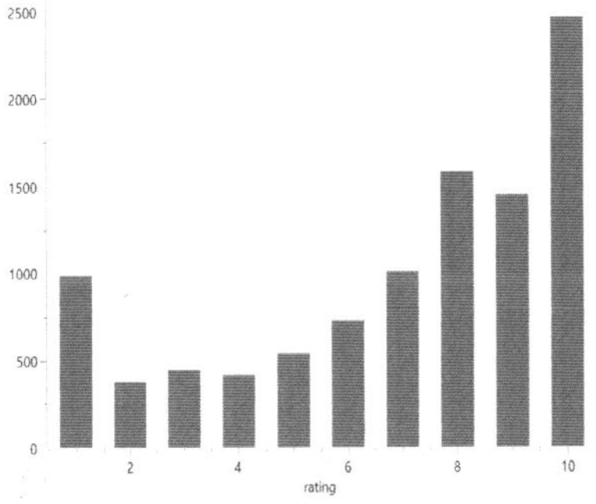

Figure 3: Distribution of labels in the dataset

functions were tested for this, namely: (1) splitting the sentiment score space into 10 equal intervals and use that as a basis to calculate the regression (Linear); (2) create intervals proportional to the frequency of each review score in the dataset (Frequency-Sensitive).

4.2.2. Supervised ML Approach

The SML approaches can be divided in two main steps: (i) Vectorization; (ii) Regression. The vectorization step takes the output of preprocessing and represents the documents into numeric vectors to be used by the regression algorithm. For this, we experimented with both Doc2Vec (Le and Mikolov, 2014), using *gensim*[7], and TF-IDF, using *scikit-learn*[8], which were fit to the training set. For the regression, we opted for Support Vector Regression (SVR), available in *scikit-learn*, because it is a popular option for this purpose in the literature (Yasen and Tedmori, 2019; Baid et al., 2017a; Baid et al., 2017b), particularly in the prediction of movie review scores (Kapukaranov and Nakov, 2015).

4.2.3. Hybrid Approach

For the hybrid approach, SVR is also used, but in can be trained in: polarities obtained from the lexicon; the previous concatenated to the document embedding. Token aggregation and embedding methods are chosen according to the best results of the pure lexicon and SML approaches.

4.3. Algorithm Parameters

For SVR, the C and $epsilon$ hyperparameters were tuned. For C, tested values ranged from 2^{-3} to 2^4, and for $epsilon$, from 0 to 4.
For Doc2Vec, we experimented with different vector sizes to conclude that 200 was the one to used. We also experimented with 10, 100, 200 and 500 training epochs. For TF-IDF, we cut the maximum number of features produced by the algorithm, as there were close to 40,000 different tokens across all text documents. We experimented with keeping only the 500, 1000, 1500 and 2000 most important tokens.

4.4. Evaluation Metrics

We compare the performance of the different approaches on the evaluation set, mentioned earlier. Performance is evaluated in terms of Mean Squared Error (MSE), Mean Absolute Error (MAE) and Pearson Correlation (ρ) between the predicted and the gold rating.

5. Experimentation and Results

For each family of approach, at least one experiment was made in order to determine which is the best. For SML, multiple experiments were run to tune the SVR parameters and to select the best embedding method, between Doc2Vec and TF-IDF.
As for the lexicon approach, we measured the performance of the algorithm based on the lexicon, the token aggregation function, the sentiment aggregation function, and the mapping function. Experiments were made using EON, but also OntoSenticNet alone.
For the hybrid approach, we selected the best performing methods in the lexicon and SML approaches. Experiments with and without the use of vectorization were also conducted.

5.1. Lexicon Approach

We conducted the pairwise analysis of the lexicon approach for each variable, but for the sake of presenting

[7] https://radimrehurek.com/gensim/
[8] https://scikit-learn.org/

the acquired information in a digestible way, we analyse each variable individually. First, we analyse the impact of the token aggregation option on performance, reported in Table 2. This was computed with EON, the frequency-sensitive mapping function and, since we needed a document score for computing the metrics, the Mean was used for sentence aggregation. For all metrics, the best performance was achieved with the Neg 4 aggregation, suggesting that negative opinions are more important for the sentence sentiment. Following this, we decided to use Neg 4 for token aggregation in further experimentation.

Table 2: MSE, MAE, Correlation based on the token aggregation function

Token Aggr.	MAE	MSE	ρ
Mean	2.428	10.068	0.170
Max	2.453	10.190	0.130
Max 3	2.427	10.457	0.217
Max 5	2.420	10.107	0.227
Neg 2	2.402	9.536	0.214
Neg 3	2.404	9.351	0.206
Neg 4	**2.395**	**9.017**	**0.244**

We then analysed sentence aggregation. Table 3 reports the performance for each option, using Neg 4 for token aggregation and EON. Here, Max 5 achieved slightly better results in MAE and ρ, while Neg 4 got a better MSE. As the differences were low, we decided to opt also for Neg 4 for sentence aggregation.

Table 3: MSE, MAE, Correlation based on the Sentence aggregation function

Sentence Aggr.	MAE	MSE	ρ
Mean	2.394	9.087	0.226
Max	2.452	9.502	0.186
Max 3	2.390	9.173	0.238
Max 5	**2.389**	9.042	**0.247**
Neg 2	2.400	8.835	0.247
Neg 3	2.411	8.785	0.242
Neg 4	2.421	**8.775**	0.237

After selecting both the token and sentence aggregation methods, we used them for checking whether the created lexicon, EON, was a better option than OntoSenticNet. The figures in Table 4 show that EON performs better, confirming the benefits of using a larger lexicon, resulting from the combination of two slightly different, possibly complementary, ones.

Table 4: MSE, MAE, Correlation based on the lexicon

Lexicon	MAE	MSE	ρ
OntoSenticNet	2.443	9.640	0.211
EON	**2.421**	**8.775**	**0.237**

Lastly, we examined the performance of the two functions proposed for mapping sentiment values (0–1) to the review score (1–10). Figures in Table 5 show that, for all metrics, the Frequency-Sensitive function leads to a substantially better performance than the Linear.

Table 5: MSE, MAE, Correlation based on the mapping function.

Mapping	MAE	MSE	ρ
Linear	3.177	12.880	0.177
Freq.-Sensitive	**2.421**	**8.775**	**0.237**

Following the experiments with the lexicon, these were our main decisions:

- When aggregating both token sentiment in sentence scores and sentence scores into document scores, negative sentiment scores are weighted four times more than positive (Neg 4). The effectiveness of this option can be the consequence of an imbalance in the lexicons, especially in OntoSenticNet, where positive terms are abundant and many seemingly neutral terms (e.g., "frequent" or "pick") have high positive scores.
- EON is a better option than OntoSenticNet alone. Including information from two different sources of knowledge enables to compute polarities that better reflect the real sentiment connotation of each word. This provides empirical evidence that the creation of broader sentiment lexicons, by merging already available ones, is effective.
- To map from the 0–1 interval that the approaches output to the 1–10 of the reviews, use a frequency-sensitive mapping function instead of its linear counterpart. This makes sense because the distribution of the review scores in the dataset is not linear, being more skewed towards the middling values of the scale.

5.2. Supervised ML Approach

Figure 4 shows the variation of MSE for different values of the SVR hyperparameters, C and $epsilon$, in experiments using Doc2Vec (left), with 10, 200 and 500 epochs, or TF-IDF (right), with 500, 1000 and 2000 maximum features.

Increasing the number of epochs leads to lower MSE for the majority of the SVR parameters. On the other hand, the increase from 200 to 500 does not lead to improvements. For TF-IDF, increasing the number of features helps to decrease MSE slightly. Specifically, going from 500 to 1000 features improves the performance more clearly than from 1000 to 2000, where it seems to almost stagnate. As for the best SVR parameterization, we can see that the best results are obtained with $C > 2$ and $epsilon$ between 0 and 1.

Figure 5 compares TF-IDF and Doc2Vec with the best parameters obtained previously (2000 and 200 respectively). Overall, they seem to perform equally in the best case scenarios, while for parameters where the performance degrades, the errors of Doc2Vec are lower.

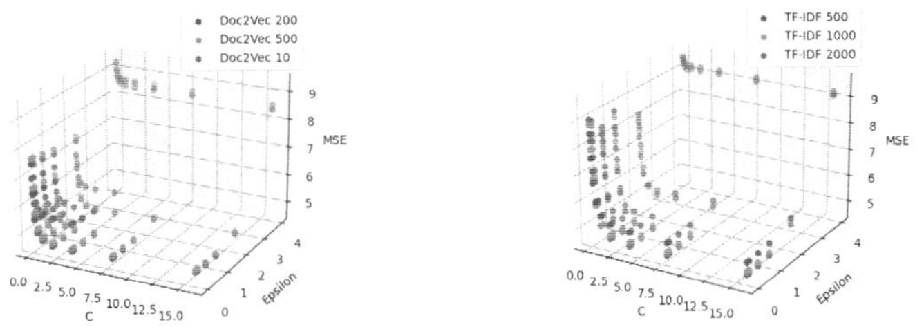

Figure 4: MSE for Doc2Vec and TF-IDF for multiple SVR parameters in the cross-validation set.

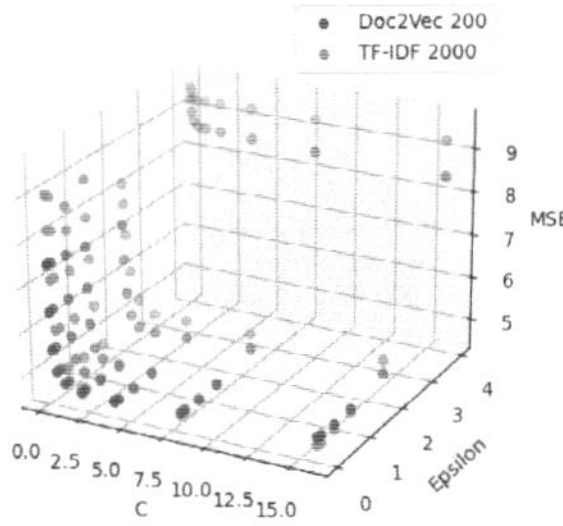

Figure 5: Comparison of the best parameters of Doc2Vec and TF-IDF in the cross-validation set.

Table 6 summarizes the best results obtained for Doc2Vec and TF-IDF in terms of MSE, MAE and ρ. While MSE is the same as in Figure 5, here it is possible to observe similar results for MAE and ρ, where both embedding methods obtain close results, even if TF-IDF has a slight advantage.

Table 6: MSE, MAE, Correlation for embedding method in the cross-validation set.

C/Epsilon	Emb.	MAE	MSE	ρ
4/0.01	Doc2Vec	1.694	4.691	0.684
4/0.01	TF-IDF	1.688	4.662	0.687

Based on the previous results, we set $C = 4$ and $epsilon = 0.01$ for the SVR. For the embedding, we opted for 200 epochs for Doc2Vec and 2,000 maximum features for TF-IDF. With these parameters, the approaches were tested in the evaluation set, with results in Table 7.

Table 7: MSE, MAE, Correlation for the embedding method in the evaluation set

C/Epsilon	Emb.	MAE	MSE	Corr.
4/0.01	Doc2Vec	1.953	5.879	0.623
4/0.01	TF-IDF	1.712	4.886	0.686

The difference in performance between both embedding approaches becomes more apparent in the evaluation set. While TF-IDF achieves a similar performance to cross-validation, Doc2Vec increases MAE and MSE significantly. TF-IDF is therefore be the embedding method used in the hybrid approach experiments. Following the experiments with the SML approach, we have the following observations:

- When using Doc2Vec, we were expecting a positive correlation between performance and the number of training epochs. Indeed, 200 epochs leads to a lower error in regression than 10, but also than 500, which might be a consequence of overfitting to the training dataset.

- For TF-IDF, the more features are considered, the lower the error.

- Even though both embedding options performed similarly in cross-validation, this did not hold up in the evaluation set. This suggests that, by using a larger representation, TF-IDF is able to better embed a more varied set of documents.

- The SVR is used with the following hyperparameters: $C = 4$ and $epsilon = 0.01$.

5.3. Hybrid Approach

The hybrid approach combines the lexicon and SML approaches, using the best parameters for each, selected after the results of the previous sections. Four hybrid configurations were tested, where different document representations were used with the SVR, namely: EON sentiment values (Tok.); EON sentiment values concatenated to the TF-IDF vector (Tok. + TF-IDF); sentence sentiment scores, obtained with the Neg 4 function (Sent.); and sentence sentiment scores concatenated to the TF-IDF vector (Sent. + TF-IDF). In each of those experiments, zero padding was applied in order to assure equal input size. This procedure was required because sentences with different number of tokens, and reviews with different number of sentences, cause discrepancies in instance input size. Table 8 shows the results obtained.

Table 8: MSE, MAE, Correlation for the Hybrid Approaches in the cross-validation set.

C/Eps.	Method	MAE	MSE	ρ
0.5/1	Tok.	2.357	8.729	0.127
4/0.01	Tok. + TF-IDF	1.726	4.871	0.670
0.5/1	Sent.	2.318	8.848	0.211
4/0.01	Sent. + TF-IDF	1.666	4.630	0.691

Figures show that the vector representation is fundamental for a good performance, as without them it would not be much different from the lexicon approach. The sentence sentiment score also leads to better results than the polarity values extracted directly from the lexicon. As such, using as input the sentence sentiment score and the vector representation showed to be the best hybrid approach.

Following this, the best hybrid approaches were tested in the evaluation set, with results in Table 9. As it happened in the cross-validation, the best results are achieved with sentence + TF-IDF. However, the performance of both degrades, especially for Token + TF-IDF.

Table 9: MSE, MAE, Correlation for the Hybrid Approaches in the evaluation set

C/Eps.	Method	MAE	MSE	Corr.
4/0.01	Tok. + TF-IDF	1.798	5.308	0.6524
4/0.01	Sent. + TF-IDF	1.699	4.879	0.686

These experiments showed that:

- There are no clear improvements between learning regression from the polarities obtained from the lexicon or applying equation 1. This was somewhat expected, following the difference between the SML and lexicon approach, implying that the vector representation has more discriminant power.
- When polarities from the lexicon are concatenated with the embedding of the documents, there are improvements, but they are minimal.
- Using the aggregated token polarity for each sentence, instead of all the individual token polarities, performed slightly better. A possible cause is the increase of dimensionality when using all the tokens. Moreover, the number of tokens across all documents varies greatly, so the vectors must be zero padded to make the representation valid for the SVR. The same process must also be done for the sentences. However, the amount of padding is much lower, so less noise is inserted. This was backed up by the results in the evaluation set.

6. Conclusion

In this paper, we reported experiments with the three popular approaches for sentiment analysis in movie reviews: lexicon-based, supervised machine learning (SML), and hybrid approaches. In an attempt to create a more complete knowledge source for sentiment analysis, a new lexicon, EON, was created, by merging OntoSenticNet and SentiWordNet. Moreover, for each approach, experiments were made to identify the best parameters with cross-validation. The actual comparison was run in an evaluation set with data not used before. Evaluation was based on three metrics: MAE, MSE and Pearson correlation (ρ).

Out of the three approaches, hybrid yielded better results, but the difference was not substantial when compared to the SML approaches. The lexicon approach performed the worst in all metrics, mainly due to coverage and contextual issues. We further noticed that the lexicon is skewed towards positive polarities. This introduces error, making it difficult to accurately predict the true rating of the movie reviews. Overall, this behaviour matches the results found in literature (Shi et al., 2019), where pure lexicon-based approaches tend to perform worse than SML or hybrid approaches.

Despite its poor results, EON outperformed SenticNet, backing up the claim that both the size and quality of the lexicon is of extreme importance. As such, we believe that it would be important to repeat the experiment with a better lexicon, more relevant to the context of movie reviews.

SML, based on SVR, performed much better, confirming that there is more information to be extracted in the raw data than in the lexicons, as the bias towards positive tokens is not present in the vector embedding.

The hybrid approach lead only to minor improvements. This may be due to: (i) the information provided by the lexicons is flawed, as mentioned previously; (ii) traditional SML models, like an SVR, are not ideal for this kind of analysis, as the dimensionality of the data is very large and finding relations between tokens can be too complex for this model.

It is also worth noting that hybrid approaches that only use sentiment values from the lexicons perform similarly to the pure lexicon approaches, further backing up the hypothesis that content features are essential, and that lexicon scores are flawed representations of the true sentiment value of the tokens, or at least not suitable for the movie review domain. Finally, even though the errors are high considering the scale used for all approaches, supervised and hybrid approaches have relatively high correlation, indicating that, at least, the relative order of the predicted ratings is close to the real ones.

A natural step further would be to adopt state-of-the-art approaches for sentiment analysis, and text classification in general. The focus would, of course, be on deep neural networks, specifically RNNs (Tang et al., 2015) or Transformers, possibly starting with pre-trained language models (Yin et al., 2020), which should achieve better results and would allow for a better consideration of the contexts where words are used.

7. Bibliographical References

Agarwal, B., Mittal, N., Bansal, P., and Garg, S. (2015). Sentiment analysis using common-sense and context information. *Computational intelligence and neuroscience*, 2015:715730, 03.

Baid, P., Gupta, A., and Chaplot, N. (2017a). Sentiment analysis of movie reviews using machine learning techniques. *International Journal of Computer Applications*, 179:45–49, 12.

Baid, P., Gupta, A., and Chaplot, N. (2017b). Sentiment analysis of movie reviews using machine learning techniques. *International Journal of Computer Applications*, 179:45–49, 12.

Bhoir, P. and Kolte, S. (2015). Sentiment analysis of movie reviews using lexicon approach. In *2015 IEEE International Conference on Computational Intelligence and Computing Research (ICCIC)*, pages 1–6.

Cambria, E., Speer, R., Havasi, C., and Hussain, A. (2010). SenticNet: A publicly available semantic resource for opinion mining. In *AAAI Fall Symposium: Commonsense Knowledge*, volume FS-10-02 of *AAAI Technical Report*. AAAI.

Cernian, A., Sgârciu, V., and Martin, B. (2015). Sentiment analysis from product reviews using sentiwordnet as lexical resource. *2015 7th International Conference on Electronics, Computers and Artificial Intelligence (ECAI)*, pages WE–15–WE–18.

Church, K. and Hanks, P. (2002). Word association norms, mutual information, and lexicography. *Computational Linguistics*, 16, 07.

Denecke, K. (2008). Using sentiwordnet for multilingual sentiment analysis. *2008 IEEE 24th International Conference on Data Engineering Workshop*, pages 507–512.

Esuli, A. and Sebastiani, F. (2006). SentiWordNet: A publicly available lexical resource for opinion mining. In *Proceedings of the Fifth International Conference on Language Resources and Evaluation (LREC'06)*, Genoa, Italy, May. ELRA.

Habimana, O., Li, Y., Li, R., Gu, X., and Yu, G. (2020). Sentiment analysis using deep learning approaches: an overview. *Science China Information Sciences*, 63(1):1–36.

Hu, M. and Liu, B. (2004). Mining and summarizing customer reviews. In *Proceedings of the Tenth ACM SIGKDD International Conference on Knowledge Discovery and Data Mining*, KDD '04, page 168–177, New York, NY, USA. Association for Computing Machinery.

Hutto, C. and Gilbert, E. (2014). Vader: A parsimonious rule-based model for sentiment analysis of social media text. *Proceedings of the International AAAI Conference on Web and Social Media*, 8(1):216–225, May.

Jovanoski, D., Pachovski, V., and Nakov, P. (2015). Sentiment analysis in twitter for macedonian. In *Proceedings of the International Conference Recent Advances in Natural Language Processing*, pages 249–257.

Kapukaranov, B. and Nakov, P. (2015). Fine-grained sentiment analysis for movie reviews in Bulgarian. In *Proceedings of the International Conference Recent Advances in Natural Language Processing*, pages 266–274, Hissar, Bulgaria, sep. INCOMA Ltd. Shoumen, BULGARIA.

Keerthi Kumar, H. M., Harish, B. S., and Darshan, H. (2018). Sentiment analysis on imdb movie reviews using hybrid feature extraction method. *International Journal of Interactive Multimedia and Artificial Intelligence*, InPress:1, 01.

Kim, S.-M. and Hovy, E. (2004). Determining the sentiment of opinions. In *Proceedings of the 20th International Conference on Computational Linguistics*, COLING '04, page 1367–es, USA. ACL.

Kim, Y. J., Cheong, Y. G., and Lee, J. H. (2019). Prediction of a movie's success from plot summaries using deep learning models. In *Proceedings of the Second Workshop on Storytelling*, pages 127–135, Florence, Italy, August. ACL.

Le, Q. and Mikolov, T. (2014). Distributed representations of sentences and documents. In *Proceedings of the 31st International Conference on International Conference on Machine Learning - Volume 32*, ICML'14, pages II–1188–II–1196. JMLR.org.

Lobo, V. and Pandya, B. (2019). Sentiment analysis of Twitter data to predict the performance of movies. In *International Conference on Intelligent Systems and Communication Networks*.

Maas, A. L., Daly, R. E., Pham, P. T., Huang, D., Ng, A. Y., and Potts, C. (2011). Learning word vectors for sentiment analysis. In *Proceedings of the 49th Annual Meeting of the Association for Computational Linguistics: Human Language Technologies*, pages 142–150, Portland, Oregon, USA, June. Association for Computational Linguistics.

Miller, G., Beckwith, R., Fellbaum, C., Gross, D., and Miller, K. (1991). Introduction to wordnet: An online lexical database*. 3, 01.

Neethu, M. and Rajasree, R. (2013). Sentiment analysis in Twitter using machine learning techniques. pages 1–5, 07.

Pal, A., Barigidad, A., and Mustafi, A. (2020). Identifying movie genre compositions using neural networks and introducing genrec-a recommender system based on audience genre perception. In *2020 5th International Conference on Computing, Communication and Security (ICCCS)*, pages 1–7. IEEE.

Pang, B. and Lee, L. (2005). Seeing stars: Exploiting class relationships for sentiment categorization with respect to rating scales. In *Proceedings of the 43rd Annual Meeting on Association for Computational Linguistics*, ACL '05, page 115–124, USA. ACL.

Pang, B., Lee, L., and Vaithyanathan, S. (2002). Thumbs up? sentiment classification using machine learning techniques. In *Proceedings of the*

2002 Conference on Empirical Methods in Natural Language Processing (EMNLP 2002), pages 79–86. ACL.

Peters, M. E., Neumann, M., Iyyer, M., Gardner, M., Clark, C., Lee, K., and Zettlemoyer, L. (2018). Deep contextualized word representations. *CoRR*, abs/1802.05365.

Poria, S., Cambria, E., Winterstein, G., and Huang, G.-B. (2014). Sentic patterns: Dependency-based rules for concept-level sentiment analysis. *Knowledge-Based Systems*, 69:45–63.

Rosenthal, S., Farra, N., and Nakov, P. (2017). SemEval-2017 task 4: Sentiment analysis in Twitter. In *Proceedings of the 11th International Workshop on Semantic Evaluation (SemEval-2017)*, pages 502–518, Vancouver, Canada, August. ACL.

Schuller, B. and Knaup, T. (2010). Learning and knowledge-based sentiment analysis in movie review key excerpts. In *Proceedings of the Third COST 2102 International Training School Conference on Toward Autonomous, Adaptive, and Context-Aware Multimodal Interfaces: Theoretical and Practical Issues*, page 448–472, Berlin, Heidelberg. Springer-Verlag.

Shi, Y., Zhu, L., Li, W., Guo, K., and Zheng, Y. (2019). Survey on classic and latest textual sentiment analysis articles and techniques. *International Journal of Information Technology & Decision Making*, 18(04):1243–1287.

Speer, R., Chin, J., and Havasi, C. (2016). Conceptnet 5.5: An open multilingual graph of general knowledge. *CoRR*, abs/1612.03975.

Stone, P., Bales, R., Namenwirth, J., and Ogilvie, D. (2007). The general inquirer: A computer system for content analysis and retrieval based on the sentence as a unit of information. *Behavioral Science*, 7:484 – 498, 10.

Tang, D., Qin, B., and Liu, T. (2015). Document modeling with gated recurrent neural network for sentiment classification. In *Proceedings of the 2015 Conference on Empirical Methods in Natural Language Processing*, pages 1422–1432, Lisbon, Portugal, September. ACL.

Tausczik, Y. R. and Pennebaker, J. W. (2010). The psychological meaning of words: Liwc and computerized text analysis methods. *Journal of Language and Social Psychology*, 29(1):24–54.

Vizcarra, G., Mauricio, A., and Mauricio, L. (2018). A deep learning approach for sentiment analysis in spanish tweets. In Věra Kůrková, et al., editors, *Artificial Neural Networks and Machine Learning – ICANN 2018*, pages 622–629, Cham. Springer International Publishing.

Wang, Y., Huang, M., Zhu, X., and Zhao, L. (2016). Attention-based LSTM for aspect-level sentiment classification. In *Proceedings of the 2016 Conference on Empirical Methods in Natural Language Processing*, pages 606–615, Austin, Texas, November. ACL.

Yasen, M. and Tedmori, S. (2019). Movies reviews sentiment analysis and classification. 04.

Yin, D., Meng, T., and Chang, K.-W. (2020). SentiBERT: A transferable transformer-based architecture for compositional sentiment semantics. In *Proceedings of the 58th Annual Meeting of the Association for Computational Linguistics*, pages 3695–3706, Online, July. ACL.

Proceedings of the SALLD-2 Workshop @LREC2020, pages 19–24
Language Resources and Evaluation Conference (LREC 2022), Marseille, 24 June 2022

Evaluating a New Danish Sentiment Resource: the Danish Sentiment Lexicon, DSL

Nina Skovgaard Schneidermann and Bolette Sandford Pedersen
Centre for Language Technology, University of Copenhagen
Emil Holms Kanal 2, DK2300 S
ninasc@hum.ku.dk, bspedersen@hum.ku.dk

Abstract

In this paper, we evaluate a new sentiment lexicon for Danish, the Danish Sentiment Lexicon (DSL), to gain input regarding how to carry out the final adjustments of the lexicon. A feature of the lexicon that differentiates it from other sentiment resources for Danish is that it is linked to a large number of other Danish lexical resources via the DDO lemma and sense inventory and the LLOD via the Danish wordnet, DanNet. We perform our evaluation on four datasets labeled with sentiments. In addition, we compare the lexicon against two existing benchmarks for Danish: the Afinn and the Sentida resources. We observe that DSL performs mostly comparably to the existing resources, but that more fine-grained explorations need to be done in order to fully exploit its possibilities given its linking properties.

Keywords: sentiment analysis, sentiment lexicons, Danish language resources, linguistic linked open data (LLOD)

1. Introduction

As a result of the constantly growing availability of unstructured data, sentiment analysis continues to be of great interest to NLP researchers and industries alike (Liu, 2012). Recent advances in natural language processing have focused on fine-tuning large pre-trained language models such as BERT to the sentiment analysis task, enabling models to automatically extract critical features seen during training (Catelli et al., 2022). Although such approaches yield impressive results, they also tend to be notably data-hungry and may be less flexible for domain-specific tasks (Asghar et al., 2017) and low-resource languages with notable data scarcity (Eskevich et al., 2022).

A complementary method to machine learning approaches is lexicon-based sentiment analysis (Devitt and Ahmad, 2013; Khoo and Johnkhan, 2018): Lexicon or dictionary-based approaches typically make use of a word list containing individual words and matching scores aggregated over a unit of text in a dataset, cf. (Liu, 2012) among others, along with enhancement rules to the scoring mechanism that lifts the model over a simple bag-of-words approach, namely practices for reversal of the sentiment triggered by negation, and for modification of sentiment scores through intensification (Asghar et al., 2017). Although lexicon-based approaches have several limitations in practice, they have the advantage of drawing on information relevant to the domain or the characteristic of the language (Catelli et al., 2022). As such, sentiment word lists can be valuable for low-resource languages, see for instance in Enevoldsen and Hansen (2017) for Danish, where they can either be implemented in a purely rule-based model or as part of a hybrid approach; e.g., sentiment scores from lexica could function as features to a pre-trained language model or a text classifier.

Together with the focus on constructing language-specific sentiment resources, increased attention has also been given in recent years to standardizing and combining such resources, as well as with other linguistic resources as envisaged by the Linguistic Linked Data Community (LLOD), cf. `https://linguistic-lod.org/`. Iglesias and Sánchez-Rada (2021) accounts for the potential of employing standardized formats and tagsets for sentiment resources and making them interoperable and interlinked to an extent where they can be integrated with other NLP datasets and tools and applied together at a large scale.

This paper details the evaluation of a new sentiment lexicon for Danish (Nimb et al., 2022). DSL differs from the existing Danish lexica. It is linked to many other Danish lexical resources via the lemma and sense inventory of the Danish monolingual dictionary (DDO) and the LLOD via the Danish wordnet, DanNet. The evaluation includes a comparison against two existing benchmarks for Danish, namely the Afinn (Nielsen, 2020) and Sentida word lists (Lauridsen et al., 2019), and a more detailed investigation of the DSL resource. Our aim with this paper is twofold: First, we hope to provide input on how to carry out further adjustments to the resource, and secondly, we hope to more generally understand how DSL's linking with other resources contributes to the results. We hypothesize that DSL will perform better than the existing Danish benchmarks due to being more expansive than existing Danish sentiment lists.

The structure of the remaining paper is as follows: In Section 2, we present existing sentiment resources for Danish, and we then go into more detail about the new lexicon and describe its basis on lexicographical principles and linking to other resources. Section 3 describes the pre-processing and implementation steps taken to enhance the lexicon. Section 4 is a comparative evaluation of the three existing word lists, detailing obtained results and more in-depth analyses of the findings. Section 5 discusses the findings in the context of future research, and section 6 contains a summary and conclusions.

2. Relevant Background on Danish Sentiment Lexica

2.1. Existing Danish Sentiment Resources

To our knowledge, Afinn was the first freely available sentiment resource for Danish and is described together with other resources in Nielsen (2020). This sentiment list is a translation and customization of an existing English sentiment lexicon (Nielsen, 2011). The coverage amounts to approx. three thousand lemmas marked with binary polarity values indicate a polarity scale from -5 to $+5$. The resource contains no neutral words.

The more recent and slightly larger sentiment list, Sentida (Lauridsen et al., 2019), contains 5,200 word stems. A background resource for this list was constituted by a list of the 10,000 most frequent Danish words [1], of which all polarity words were selected and neutral words omitted. The list subsumes the words from Afinn and follows the same polarity scaling (-5 to $+5$).

2.2. The New Sentiment Lexicon, DSL, Integrated with other Danish Resources and with the LLOD

The Danish Sentiment Lexicon (Nimb et al., 2022) (henceforth DSL) is a recently published resource based on existing Danish dictionaries, primarily the Danish Thesaurus (Nimb et al., 2014) (henceforth DT). The work is compiled in collaboration between The Danish Society for Language and Literature and The Centre for Language Technology at the University of Copenhagen and funded by The Carlsberg Foundation. The dictionary contains 14,000 lemmas encoded with polarity values from -3 to $+3$, the lowest indicating negative and highest positive values. Less than two-thirds of the words have negative polarity, leaving the rest with positive polarity values. Furthermore, the resource includes morphosyntactic information, namely word classes and a list of word forms for each lemma. This information is not available in either Afinn or Sentida: Afinn contains only word forms, making the number of unique words notably smaller than the actual size of the word list, and Sentida includes words that have been automatically stemmed with the Danish snowball stemmer, which contains some limitations.

The primary purpose of compiling yet another sentiment lexicon for Danish was twofold.

First of all, the development was based on the hypothesis that a higher quality resource could be achieved if it was compiled using monolingual lexicographic methods and resources and not biased by an English source. More specifically, this assumption resulted in DSL being based on the links between groups of words listed in semantic order in a Danish thesaurus, DT (cf. (Nimb et al., 2022) and (Nimb et al., 2014)), and on the corresponding word sense descriptions found in a comprehensive monolingual dictionary, namely The Danish Dictionary, DDO. In short, this meant to identify negative and positive sections in the Thesaurus, extract the words from these sections and combine them with the dictionary information via links. Via the individual thematic areas of DT, the encoders of DSL had available information about synonyms and near-synonyms within a particular topic - also across word classes. The claim is that this background material further eased the calibration of polarity values across word classes and different semantic fields.

Secondly, by being integrated with a collection of Danish lexical resources, the DSL is also being linked to LLOD via the Danish wordnet, DanNet, which has recently been transformed to the Ontolex-Lemon format (Buitelaar et al., 2013). Several RDF polarity relations based on the Marl ontology (`http://www.gsi.upm.es:9080/ontologies/marl/` are defined, and all sentiment data from DSL is made available through the wordnet, with the polarity values percolated down at synset level [2]. This integration with LLOD opens for more extensive use of the sentiment data to be applied in a broader NLP pipeline where other levels of linguistic analysis are compiled and where textual data sets and similar resources for other languages can be taken into account. Combining cross-lingual data with purely monolingually defined data in DSL could potentially improve the usability of the resource.

3. Experiments

Our experiments consisted of implementing a model and evaluating it against existing benchmarks on four manually annotated sentiment datasets, all of which were made publically available through the DaNLP repository (Pauli et al., 2021). The datasets are as follows:

- EuroparlSentiment1. It consists of 184 sentences from sections of the Danish part of the Europarl Corpus (Koehn, 2005). The sentences are manually annotated with polarity scores between -3 and 3 by Nielsen (2020)

[1]The list was achieved from The Danish Society for Language and Literature: `https://korpus.dsl.dk/resources/details/freq-lemmas.html`

[2]Note that DSL was encoded with a basis in the DDO and therefore originally encoded at sense level. Lemmas that had several senses with diverging polarity were carefully studied. Half of these were rejected due to ambiguity (e.g., frelst ('saved'), sej ('tough'), skarp ('sharp'), overlegen ('superior') and glat ('smooth'). The other half was kept in the lexicon since it was estimated that the polarity sense was by far the most frequent sense of the lemma (Nimb et al., 2022)

- LCCsentiment: Consists of 499 sentences from sections of the Leipzig Corpora Collection (henceforth LCC) (Biemann et al., 2007), likewise annotated by Nielsen (2020) in the same way as Europarl1.

- EuroparlSentiment2. It consists of additional 957 sentences from Europarl annotated by the Alexandra Institute (Pauli et al., 2021). The dataset contains both subjectivity and polarity scores, although only polarity values are measured in this instance. Polarity values are annotated as 'negative', 'positive', or 'neutral'.

- TwitterSentiment. It consists of 1413 tweets annotated by the Alexandra Institute with negative, positive, and neutral polarity labels (Pauli et al., 2021).

Our model implementation consists of a search function that matches the lexicon against the dataset to be searched and a scoring function that aggregates the sentiment scores over every sentence in the dataset. The following sections will describe the pre-processing steps on the data, along with additional rules and enhancements implemented to increase the scoring accuracy. Finally, the measures of evaluation are briefly discussed.

3.1. Pre-processing

Before the search is conducted, the data is tokenized and POS-tagged using DaCy as a pre-processing step. This Danish pre-processing framework has achieved state-of-the-art performance on POS-tagging and named entity recognition (Enevoldsen et al., 2021). The data is then lemmatized with tokens and POS-tags as inputs using Lemmy [3], a python-based Danish lemmatizer trained on the Danish full-form list from DDO and the Universal Dependencies converted from the Danish Dependency Treebank (DDT) (Johannsen et al., 2015). This step was taken to utilize the morphosyntactic information available in DSL, word classes, and homographs, to disambiguate words in the data when possible (see 3.2.). It, therefore, provides an example of how linguistically linked data has been employed to increase the flexibility of our model.

Furthermore, a stopword filter was applied to the tokens to decrease noise during scoring. We made a manual assessment of the subset of the 219 words in the original stopword list, which would be useful for sentiment scoring, consisting of adverbial modifiers 3.2. along with six lemmas, primarily adverbs, which were present in DSL:

- 'Måske' ('maybe'): -1

- 'Nemlig' ('in fact'): 2

- 'Skulle' ('have to', 'should'): -1

[3]See https://github.com/sorenlind/lemmy

- 'Alene' ('alone'): -1

- 'God' ('good'): 3

- 'Allerede' ('already'): 1

Conversely, the stopword list also included instances of words that were present in DSL but which have ambiguity issues that can currently not be solved: An example of this is 'du,' which in Danish is ambiguous between the 2nd person singular pronoun and the infinitive form of the verb 'to function.' Since there is currently no implementation to effectively deal with cases where a sentiment-bearing word is ambiguous with a frequent, non-sentiment-bearing word, the presence of the lemma would contribute to more noise than useful information during the search and was therefore filtered out.

3.2. Model enhancements

Our enhancement rules consist of two components: Disambiguation rules in cases of homographs and sentiment-modifying rules in the presence of negators and intensifiers.

DSL is the only one of the three lists containing homographs, i.e., duplicate sentiment-bearing lemmas with different meanings and sense-level information and parts of speech from DDO. This makes it possible to implement simple disambiguation procedures in cases where sentiment-bearing homographs were found during matching: For this purpose, we map the part-of-speech information in DSL to the automatic POS tags generated by DaCy and match them against the data. If a matching POS tag is found for a given ambiguous lemma, the model chooses the corresponding sentiment score and drops the remaining ones. Otherwise, it takes the 1st sense of the word in DDO to be the correct one, as this is typically also the most frequent.[4]

Additionally, a series of heuristics (Lauridsen et al., 2019) for dealing with sentiment-modifying elements were applied: Sentiment scores are reversed in the presence of negation if a sentiment-bearing word exists within the scope of -1 to $+3$ positions from the negation trigger. Other elements that have been found to increase or reduce sentiment include intensifying adverbial modifiers ('very,' èxtremely,' 'slightly' etc.), the conjunct 'but,' which could be said to weaken the statement expressed by the preceding clause, and exclamation marks and all-caps, which both increase the score (Dragut and Fellbaum, 2014; Asghar et al., 2017). We applied a dictionary of adverbial modifiers and their corresponding values, which were initially described for English by (Dragut and Fellbaum, 2014) and adjusted for Danish by Lauridsen et al. (2019). The values are multiplied with the total sentiment score if an adverbial modifier is proceeded by a sentiment-bearing word.

[4]It should be noted that the SpaCy POS-tags are not in one-to-one correspondence with the word classes in DDO, which may contribute to some inaccuracies.

3.3. Evaluation

The three resources were evaluated using two different metrics: First, we calculated the Pearson rank correlation coefficients between a given lexicon and the human-annotated sentiment scores for each dataset. Secondly, we divided the scores outputted by DSL for each dataset into negative, neutral, and positive classes following the procedure for existing DaNLP sentiment benchmarks [5]. This enabled a more direct evaluation of the datasets annotated with 3-way polarity. To account for the imbalance towards words with negative polarity in DSL (62 %), we trained a logistic regression classifier on 990 examples of the TwitterSentiment dataset and adjusted the optimal threshold value, which is given by $max(tpr - fpr)$, where tpr denotes the true positive rate and fpr the false positive rate (Flach, 2010). In accordance with the procedure described by (Pauli et al., 2021), neutral class is taken to be on a continuum rather than a discrete value. Thus, we set the threshold to 0.37 and take scores between -0.37 and 0.37 to belong to the neutral class, scores above 0.37 to be positive, and scores below -0.37 to be negative.

4. Results and analyses

Table 1 provides an overview of the results of the comparative evaluation on each dataset. Table 2 reports on the recall, precision, and micro F1-score for the negative, neutral, and positive classes on DSL.

Dataset	Lexicon	Corr.	Acc.	Avg. F1	Wgt. F1
Europarl1	DSL	**0.703**	**0.685**	0.675	0.676
	Sentida	0.671	0.669	0.651	0.657
	Afinn	0.634	**0.685**	**0.676**	**0.681**
LCC	DSL	0.512	0.639	0.593	0.639
	Sentida	0.526	0.581	0.548	0.579
	Afinn	0.516	0.655	0.606	0.652
Europarl2	DSL	0.459	0.543	0.533	0.541
	Sentida	0.473	0.533	0.514	0.527
	Afinn	0.413	0.557	0.547	0.560
Twitter-Sentiment	DSL	0.387	0.462	0.448	0.470
	Sentida	0.396	0.423	0.416	0.424
	Afinn	0.334	0.478	0.46	0.485

Table 1: Comparative evaluation of Danish sentiment resources.

4.1. Analyses

Overall, we can observe that DSL appears to perform comparably to the existing word lists, with the most significant improvement being a Pearson correlation of 0.70 with EuroparlSentiment1 against 0.66 and 0.63 on Sentida and Afinn, respectively. However, in most cases, DSL does not perform notably better than either

Dataset	Class	Precision	Recall	F1
Europarl1	Negative	**0.781**	0.472	0.588
	Neutral	0.679	0.679	0.679
	Positive	0.634	**0.9**	**0.744**
LCC	Negative	0.474	0.383	0.424
	Neutral	0.727	0.672	0.698
	Positive	0.581	0.758	0.658
Europarl2	Negative	0.593	0.414	0.488
	Neutral	0.654	0.484	0.556
	Positive	0.43	0.768	0.551
Twitter-Sentiment	Negative	0.744	0.411	0.529
	Neutral	0.314	0.359	0.335
	Positive	0.372	0.68	0.481

Table 2: Metrics for each class in DSL on evaluated datasets.

word list; in fact, it does not exceed Afinn on classification of tweets, which may be due to the fact that Afinn contains several more colloquial phrasings specific to the domain of social media (Nielsen, 2011). We also observe notable differences between the performances for the evaluated datasets, part of which could be due to significant differences in class distributions: The neutral class in EuroparlSentiment2 comprises nearly half of the samples, whereas only about a fifth of the TwitterSentiment samples are marked as neutral. Furthermore, the overall score appears to decrease with increasing sample sizes, suggesting that the relatively high scores on EuroparlSentiment1 may be a product of few example sentences.

By examining the errors manually, however, we can learn a lot about what may contribute to the relatively minor differences between DSL and the other word lists, in spite of our hypothesis that its expansiveness would yield more reliable sentiment scores: Namely, an inspection of the 1000 most frequent words over all the datasets reveals that the proportion of matched words in DSL only comprises 260 of the 14000 lemmas, of which 225 intersect with Sentida [6]. This may indicate that although the DSL resource may be more expansive in a linguistic sense, it may not make a substantial difference in practice within the relatively conventional domain of politics, news, and social media. In fact, inspecting some of the instances of falsely rated sentiments suggests that DSL may even be too exhaustive in its attribution of sentiment: Namely, words such as 'skulle' ('should, have to') and 'sidste' ('last') are given a sentiment score of -1 and 1, respectively, although examples such as, 'parlamentet skal træffe en beslutning' ('the parlament need to make a decision'), and 'det er deres sidste chance' ('it is their last chance') suggests contexts where a more neutral attribution may be warranted. Other examples of debatable sentiments

[5] `https://github.com/alexandrainst/danlp` (Pauli et al., 2021)

[6] Note that stemming was performed on the DSL lemmas to determine this

are adverbials such as 'måske' ('maybe'), 'allerede' ('already'), and àlligevel' ('still'), which may be better suited as modifying the sentiment of a given sentence than being given their own values. A final point of observation is that DSL is the only one of the three lists containing multiple word senses, which, as seen in 3.1., can cause problems for a rudimentary analysis.

5. Discussion

The results displayed in 4. strongly suggest that a rudimentary evaluation may not be sufficient to uncover the assumed benefits of a more exhaustive sentiment lexicon, particularly with respect to its linked data properties. This is primarily because models that fully utilize the lexicon's linking to DanNet have not yet been implemented given that the resource is relatively recent. As a future line of research, it may be advantageous to investigate the effectiveness of DSL for domain-specific ontology-based approaches to sentiment analysis. The interoperability of the DSL with sense-level information from DanNet and RDF polarity relations based on the MARL ontology would potentially make the graded polarity scores valuable as linguistic features in an aspect-based sentiment model. Developing formal representations of how concepts are related within a given subdomain has been shown to improve both accuracy and flexibility of sentiment models, since it enables a fine-grained overview of public sentiment towards specific topics (García-Díaz et al., 2020). Generally, understanding how DSL may benefit domain-specific flexibility is recommended.

6. Conclusion

This paper has detailed the efforts to evaluate the new Danish Sentiment Lexicon, DSL, which is being linked to the LLOD. We experimented on 4 labelled datasets and performed rudimentary pre-processing of the data, and employed basic rules designed to lift the model slightly over a bag-of-words approach, as well as to take advantage of sense-level information provided by the lexicon. While our rudimentary analyses were not able to verify the effectiveness of DSL over other lexica, it was confirmed that DSL performs comparably with existing Danish word lists in a basic setting. However, in order to fully exploit the possibilities provided by the linking of DSL with other resources, more complex implementations need to be made, an example of which is employing the lexicon for more fine-grained ontology-based sentiment models within specific domains.

Bibliographical References

Asghar, M. Z., Khan, A., Ahmad, S., Qasim, M., and Khan, I. A. (2017). Lexicon-enhanced sentiment analysis framework using rule-based classification scheme. *PloS one*, 12(2):e0171649.

Biemann, C., Heyer, G., Quasthoff, U., and Richter, M. (2007). The leipzig corpora collection-monolingual corpora of standard size. *Proceedings of Corpus Linguistic*, 2007.

Buitelaar, P., Arcan, M., Iglesias, C. A., Sánchez-Rada, J. F., and Strapparava, C. (2013). Linguistic linked data for sentiment analysis. In *Proceedings of the 2nd Workshop on Linked Data in Linguistics (LDL-2013): Representing and linking lexicons, terminologies and other language data*, pages 1–8.

Catelli, R., Pelosi, S., and Esposito, M. (2022). Lexicon-based vs. bert-based sentiment analysis: A comparative study in italian. *Electronics*, 11(3):374.

Devitt, A. and Ahmad, K. (2013). Is there a language of sentiment? an analysis of lexical resources for sentiment analysis. *Language resources and evaluation*, 47(2):475–511.

Dragut, E. and Fellbaum, C. (2014). The role of adverbs in sentiment analysis. In *Proceedings of Frame Semantics in NLP: A Workshop in Honor of Chuck Fillmore (1929-2014)*, pages 38–41.

Enevoldsen, K. C. and Hansen, L. (2017). Analysing political biases in danish newspapers using sentiment analysis. *Journal of Language Works-Sprogvidenskabeligt Studentertidsskrift*, 2(2):87–98.

Enevoldsen, K., Hansen, L., and Nielbo, K. (2021). Dacy: A unified framework for danish nlp. *arXiv preprint arXiv:2107.05295*.

Eskevich, M., de Jong, F., Giagkou, R. M., and Hajič, J. (2022). Project european language equality (ele) grant agreement no. lc-01641480–101018166 ele coordinator prof. dr. andy way (dcu) co-coordinator prof. dr. georg rehm (dfki) start date, duration 01-01-2021, 18 months.

Flach, P. A., (2010). *ROC Analysis*, pages 869–875. Springer US, Boston, MA.

García-Díaz, J. A., Cánovas-García, M., and Valencia-García, R. (2020). Ontology-driven aspect-based sentiment analysis classification: An infodemiological case study regarding infectious diseases in latin america. *Future Generation Computer Systems*, 112:641–657.

Iglesias, C. A. and Sánchez-Rada, J. F. (2021). Sentiment analysis meets linguistic linked data. *Proceedings from SALLD-1 2021*, 2021.

Johannsen, A., Alonso, H. M., and Plank, B. (2015). Universal dependencies for danish. In *International Workshop on Treebanks and Linguistic Theories (TLT14)*, page 157.

Khoo, C. S. and Johnkhan, S. B. (2018). Lexicon-based sentiment analysis: Comparative evaluation of six sentiment lexicons. *Journal of Information Science*, 44(4):491–511.

Koehn, P. (2005). Europarl: A parallel corpus for statistical machine translation. In *Proceedings of machine translation summit x: papers*, pages 79–86.

Lauridsen, G. A., Dalsgaard, J. A., and Svendsen, L. K. B. (2019). Sentida: A new tool for sentiment analysis in danish. *Journal of Language Works-Sprogvidenskabeligt Studentertidsskrift*, 4(1):38–53.

Liu, B. (2012). Sentiment analysis and opinion mining. *Synthesis lectures on human language technologies*, 5(1):1–167.

Nielsen, F. A. (2011). A new ANEW: Evaluation of a word list for sentiment analysis in microblogs. In *Making Sense of Microposts (MSM2011), 93-98.*

Nielsen, F. A. (2020). Danish resources. Technical report, Danish Technical University, Lyngby.

Nimb, S., Lorentzen, H., Theilgaard, L., and Troelsgård, T. (2014). *Den danske begrebsordbog*. Det Danske Sprog-og Litteraturselskab.

Nimb, S., Olsen, S., Pedersen, B. S., and Troelsgaard, T. (2022). A thesaurus-based sentiment lexicon for danish: The danish sentiment lexicon. In *Proceedings of the 13th International Conference on Language Resources and Evaluation (LREC'12)*, pages 3746–3753, Marseille, France, May. European Language Resource Association (ELRA).

Pauli, A. B., Barrett, M., Lacroix, O., and Hvingelby, R. (2021). Danlp: An open-source toolkit for danish natural language processing. In *Proceedings of the 23rd Nordic Conference on Computational Linguistics (NoDaLiDa)*, pages 460–466.

Proceedings of the SALLD-2 Workshop @LREC2020, pages 25–30
Language Resources and Evaluation Conference (LREC 2022), Marseille, 24 June 2022

Correlating Environmental Facts and Social Media Trends Leveraging Commonsense Reasoning and Human Sentiments

Brad McNamee[1], Aparna S. Varde[2,3], Simon Razniewski[3]
1. Computational Linguistics Program, Montclair State University, Montclair, NJ, USA
2. Department of Computer Science, Montclair State University, Montclair, NJ, USA
3. Max Planck Institute for Informatics, Saarbrucken, Germany
mcnameeb1@montclair.edu, vardea@montclair.edu, srazniew@mpi-inf.mpg.de
(* A. Varde: Visiting Researcher at Max Planck Institute for Informatics)

Abstract

As climate change alters the physical world we inhabit, opinions surrounding this hot-button issue continue to fluctuate. This is apparent on social media, particularly Twitter. In this paper, we explore concrete climate change data concerning the Air Quality Index (AQI), and its relationship to tweets. We incorporate commonsense connotations for appeal to the masses. Earlier work focuses primarily on accuracy and performance of sentiment analysis tools / models, much geared towards experts. We present commonsense interpretations of results, such that they are not impervious to the masses. Moreover, our study uses real data on multiple environmental quantities comprising AQI. We address human sentiments gathered from linked data on hashtagged tweets with geolocations. Tweets are analyzed using VADER, subtly entailing commonsense reasoning. Interestingly, correlations between climate change tweets and air quality data vary not only based upon the year, but also the specific environmental quantity. We anticipate that this study will shed light on possible areas to increase awareness of climate change, and methods to address it, by the scientists as well as the common public. In line with Linked Data initiatives, we aim to make this work openly accessible on a network, published with the Creative Commons license.

Keywords: AQI, Commonsense Reasoning, Human Sentiments, Linked Data, Opinion Mining, Twitter Hashtags

1. Introduction

Human-caused climate change affects millions of lives. However, reactions are varied: from placing blame on other causes to speaking out against contributing factors. Our study focuses on a subset of USA Twitter users. This is pertinent because the USA has the second highest numbers of climate change deniers worldwide as evident from recent studies (Buchholz, 2020).

We address a significant area of climate change, namely, *AQI (Air Quality Index)*, and delve into multiple environmental quantities comprising this aggregated quantity. We compare this hard data to discussions around related topics represented by linked data via hashtags on Twitter. This is performed in order to glean insight into how people voice their opinions about climate change, and how various concerning issues can be analyzed from a commonsense knowledge standpoint. This is important rather than just appealing to experts (unlike much prior work) because the common public needs to take actions in order to deal with climate change, in addition to policy-makers and government bodies outling their decisions accordingly. Ideally, the purpose of this study is to enhance comprehension of where climate change education is potentially lacking, and thus propose steps to improve the concerned areas, by the masses as well as the classes.

In connection with this, we wish to mention the concept of linked data. Linked linguistic data is a current trend that focuses on making linguistic and Natural Language Processing (NLP) data openly available on a network, ideally accessible via a web browser. Likewise, an additional goal of our work is not only to associate sentiment analysis scoring with each tweet, but also to make this sentiment-analyzed-dataset available for use by others. It is our hope that it could be used in related work, pertinent to included model training or further climate change sentiment analysis, analogous to other literature (e.g. Iglesias et al., 2017). Pursuant to this goal, future work on this project will entail publishing this dataset under the Creative Commons (CC) license, ascribing it a URI, and ideally making the dataset accessible via a web interface. This would allow the data to become dynamic and easily accessible to others.

2. Related Work

Previous work touches upon this issue, though much of it focuses on adjacent areas. In an article on 'Tracking Climate Change Opinions from Twitter Data', the authors compare the performance of various sentiment analysis tools on climate change tweet data, and work towards accurately predicting sentiment and subjectivity in tweets with these tools (An et al., 2014). Some researchers perform sentiment analysis and topic modeling on climate data from cities worldwide, including Paris, London, and New Delhi. (Gurajala et al., 2019). This work is similar to ours, but focuses on a wider area but shorter time period, while also concentrating on topic modeling. A recent study (Puri et al, 2021) presents an overview of relevant topics pertaining to the COVID pandemic and social media trends surrounding it, touching upon some topics relevant to climate change as affected by the pandemic. While this study addresses many interesting aspects, it does not focus on AQI in particular, nor does it conduct a deeper analysis of the numerous quantities comprising the AQI quantity.

In another relevant study, researchers investigate similar tweet sentiments on China's well-known Weibo platform, and determine whether air quality predictions can be made by combining tweet sentiment with sparse air quality testing data from remote sensor locations in rural China (Wang et al., 2017). In a research article on 'Air Quality Assessment from Social Media and Structured Data', the authors present an insight into mining pollutant data and assessing air quality by focusing on fine particle pollutants PM2.5, i.e. particulate matter of diameter less than 2.5 microns, since these are the most dangerous (Du et al., 2016). Some researchers explore other aspects of climate change, e.g. water quality, via sentiment analyzed from created emotion dictionaries (Jiang et al., 2016).

Additionally, there are related works on commonsense knowledge with respect to its extraction and compilation (Razniewski et al., 2021), as well as its usefulness in various tasks involving machine intelligence in general (Tandon et al,, 2017). Since our study in this paper targets the common public, it is important to address issues from a commonsense angle, and accordingly derive interpretations of the inferences obtained from our analysis in this work. Hence, the commonsense perspectives are significant.

3. Approach and Experiments

We acquire AQI data from EPA (Environmental Protection Agency, USA). It has thirty air quality monitoring stations in NJ, for environmental quantities in AQI, including:

- Carbon Monoxide (CO)
- Sulfur Dioxide (SO2)
- Nitrogen Dioxide (NO2)
- Ozone (ground level)
- Particulate Matter 10 (PM10)
- Particulate Matter 2.5 (PM2.5)

This data is compiled for 14 years: 2007-2021.

We then shift focus to Twitter; using *snscrape* to harvest tweets on environmental quantities using the following criteria. The tweets need to range from 2007-2021, they should originate in NJ, and they must correspond to our accepted hashtags. Since hashtags typically serve well as linked data identifiers, we carefully select these based on commonsense knowledge as per the environment. Selected hashtags are: #airpollution, #airquality, #airqualityindex, #aqi, #cleanair, #ozone, #smog, #haze, #emissions, #pollution, #carbonmonoxide, #co, #nitrogendioxide, #no2, #sulfurdioxide, and #so2.

Some filtering is needed based on Named Entity Disambiguation, e.g., CO can imply Colorado. This is conducted while preprocessing. We compile hard data for different environmental quantities (SO2, ozone, etc.), and can visualize temporal changes. We utilize *Matplotlib* to plot each value, for AQI data and tweets.

3.1 VADER

After scraping tweets, we perform sentiment analysis via VADER (Valence Aware Dictionary and Sentiment Reasoner). It inadvertently entails commonsense reasoning through its "wisdom-of-the-crowd approach" and its manner of "establishing ground truth using aggregate data from multiple human raters" (Hutto and Gilbert, 2014). It is adept at evaluating and scoring human sentiments in social media text.

In sentiment analysis, we use the *compound* score, i.e. the normalized weighted composite of all scores, normalized between (-1, +1), thus enhancing analysis from a commonsense standpoint. If it is >=0.05, we assign the tweets a positive sentiment; if it is > -0.05 and <0.05, tweets are neutral; if it is <=-0.05, tweets are negative. (Hutto and Gilbert, 2014).

3.2 Experimental Process and Algorithm

The diagram in Figure 1 below summarizes the high-level process adapted in this study, and detailed next.

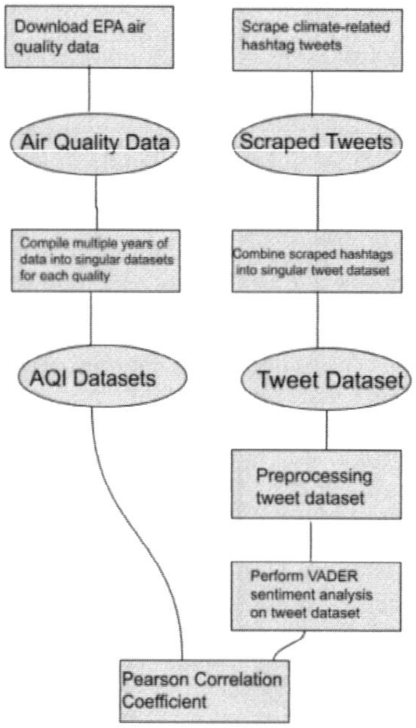

Figure 1: Overview of Experimental Process

3.3 Algorithm 1 on Compilation of AQI

We now present two succint algorithms proposed in our work. Algorithm 1 summarizes the process for finding and compiling AQI records using the EPA source. This is outlined below.

Algorithm 1 : Compile AQI records from EPA

```
FUNCTION compileAQI (EPA_record):
#Each separate AQI factor is compiled separately
AQI_Dataset_$quality = []
FOREACH year in EPA_record :
        DOWNLOAD AQI data
AQI_Dataset += EPA_record
return AQI_Dataset
```

3.4 Algorithm 2 on Acquisition of Tweets

The next algorithm, i.e. Algorithm 2, describes the process for scraping the tweets, and combining them into a singular tweet dataset. This is presented below.

Algorithm 2 : Acquire tweets and construct dataset

```
FUNCTION getTweets(list_of_hashtags) :
Tweet_Datset = []
FOREACH hashtag in list_of_hashtags :
#separate dataset for each hashtag
        Dataset_$hashtag = []
#scrape Twitter w/ snscrape for that hashtag, as well as other
#parameters
        Dataset_$hashtag += snscrape(hashtag)

FOREACH Dataset_$hashtag :
        Tweet_Datset += Dataset_$hashtag
FOREACH tweet in Tweet_Dataset :
#remove tweets that are nonlegible, nonsensical, or completely
#unrelated
        PREPROCESS tweet
FOREACH tweet in Tweet_Dataset :
        CONDUCT sentiment analysis
        ADD results of analysis to column in Tweet_Dataset
```

---

4. Results and Discussion

4.1 AQI Values and Tweet Sentiments

The results of our experiments are summarized in Figures 2-7. The tweets emanate from 2972 unique users, the most frequent ones (with 421 and 228 tweets respectively) being an industrial cooling cleaning company and a private user.

Text	Date
Everyone deserves clean air ðŸŒŽ #cleanair #AirPollution #uconn https://t.co/KHYZDmGgwB	2021-12-04
Study suggests #children w specific genetic allele may be more susceptible to neurobehavioral problems when exposed to traffic #airpollution https://t.co/q1lo1OkM2r	2019-02-16
Exposure to particulate air pollutants associated with numerous types of cancer https://t.co/BNRmYWoBfM #cancer #airpollution #cleanair #USA	2017-10-15
Come check out our brand new website! https://t.co/lLz48hwAGf ðŸŒ□. The Pandora Project is a global ground based atmospheric trace gas network. #NO2 #O3 #HCHO #SO2 #Pandora #instrument #NASA ðŸŒŽ	2020-01-28
Proud of the students in and around #District36 who have taken a stand to protect our environment. #cleanenergy #cleanair #cleanwater #NewJersey https://t.co/jH8TaV4m0c	2019-06-27

Figure 2: Sample Tweets from Dataset

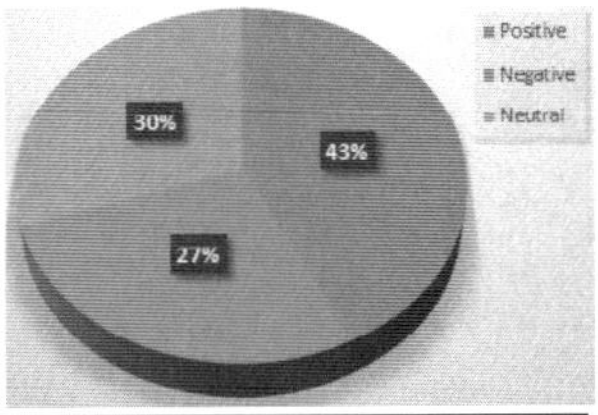

Sentiment Classification	Number of Tweets
Positive	2490
Negative	1603
Neutral	1755
Total	*5848*

Figure 3: Sentiment Distribution of Tweets

Figure 4: Word Cloud Visualization of All Terms

Figure 5 : Word Cloud Visualization of Positive Tweets

Figure 6 : Word Cloud Visualization of Negative Tweets

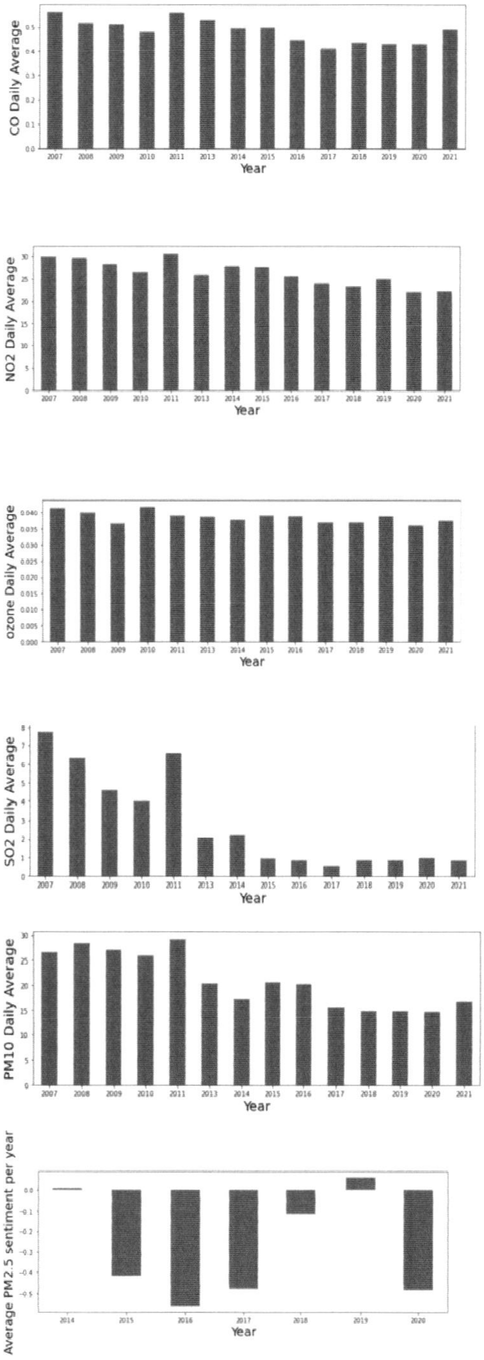

Figure 7: Average Daily Values for Quantities

Figure 2 in this paper depicts a snapshot of sample tweets from our dataset, subjected to analysis. Figure 3 illustrates the sentiment distribution of all the tweets after analysis. Figures 4, 5, and 6 present the Word Cloud Visualization of terms in all the tweets, the positive tweets, and the negative tweets, respectively. Figure 7 includes bar charts portraying the average daily values for all the quantities analyzed in the overall AQI quantity, i.e. CO, PM2.5 etc. Figure 8 comprises bar charts for the average sentiment values on the same quantities, synopsizing the analysis.

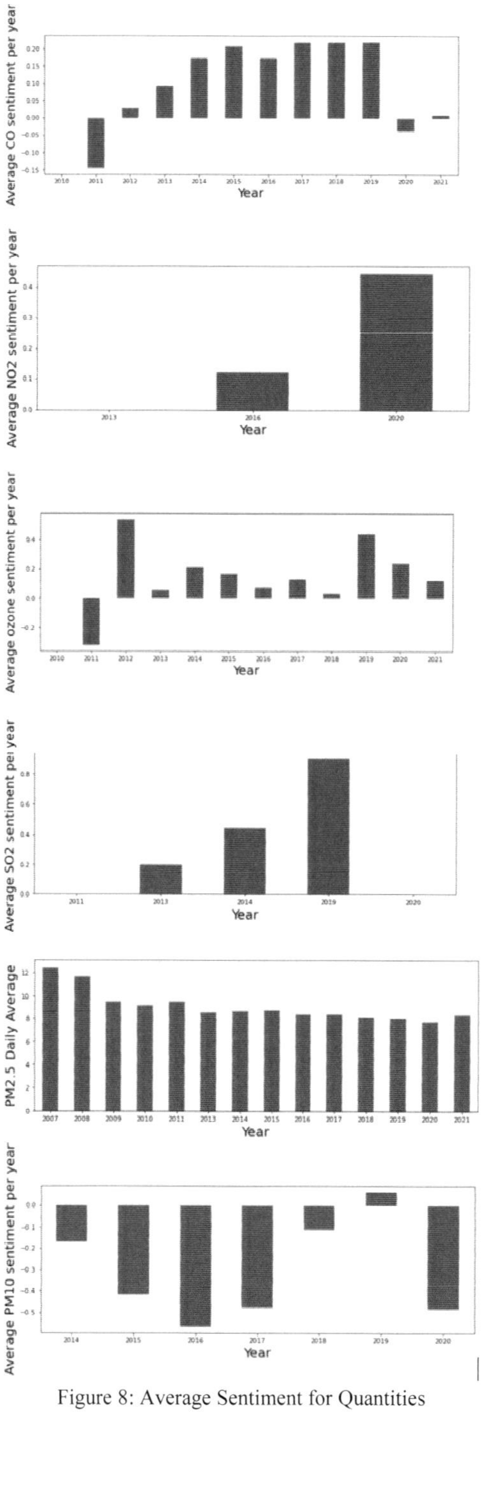

Figure 8: Average Sentiment for Quantities

4.2 Pearson's Correlation Coefficient

In order to better understand the relationship between quantity values and tweet sentiments, we utilize the Pearson's correlation coefficient (PCC). This measurement details the strength and direction of the linear association between two variables with no assumption of causality (Nickolas, 2021). The table below, i.e. Table 1, provides the names of each quantity within AQI (analyzed in our work) and the associated Pearson's Correlation Coefficient.

Quantity	Pearson's Correlation Coefficient
Ozone (ground)	0.0095
Carbon Monoxide	-0.0616
Sulfur Dioxide	-0.3489
Nitrous Dioxide	-0.3530
Particulate Matter 2.5	0.3398
Particulate Matter 10	0.1866

Table 1: Pearson's Correlation Coefficient for AQI quantities showing relationships between the actual quantity values and their respective tweet sentiments

In order to interpret the results as shown in this table, it is important to understand that a correlation coefficient >0 indicates a positive relationship between two values, while a coefficient <0 indicates a negative relationship. Additionally, if two values have a correlation coefficient >0.1 and <0.1, they are said to have no/very weak linear relationship. Finally, while this coefficient does provide unique insights, it is important to note that it is a measurement of correlation, not causality.

5. Conclusions and Roadmap

Surprisingly, most tweets have positive sentiments because people celebrate the success of climate initiatives and their own participation therein. Common climate terms (CO / ozone) have more positive sentiments than uncommon terms (PM10 / PM2.5).

Overall, we can deduce some commonsense interpretations based on human sentiments, listed as follows.

- CO, ozone, NO2, PM2.5, and PM10 depict no fluctuations in data, hence sentiment shifts in tweets must be due to other influences.
- NJ residents notice improvements in SO2 levels.
- People often tweet positively when they recognize improvements in climate change.
- The more specific / uncommon an environmental quantity is, the more negative its tweet sentiment is likely to be.

Such interpretations can enhance strategies to educate people about climate change. As future work, this can entail further questions. If people are willing to voice positive climate change work, how do we best address this through the lens of success stories? If we see more frequent usage of commonsense related climate terms (pollution, ozone), how do we harness that to strengthen climate awareness? Conversely, how can we raise awareness of less common but important aspects of AQI? Much work remains, and natural language expressions of social media can provide valuable insights into how it can be accomplished. Further investigations from commonsense standpoints can occur, leveraging the plethora of work on commonsense reasoning from sources in the literature.

6. Acknowledgements

Aparna Varde acknowledges the NSF grants 2018575 (MRI: Acquisition of a High-Performance GPU Cluster for Research & Education); and 2117308 (MRI: Acquisition of a Multimodal Collaborative Robot System (MCROS) to Support Cross- Disciplinary Human-Centered Research & Education). She is a visiting researcher at Max Planck Institute for Informatics, Saarbrucken, Germany.

7. References

An, X., Ganguly, A. R., Fang, Y., Scyphers, S. B., Hunter, A. M., and Dy, J. G. (2014). Tracking climate change opinions from twitter data, Workshop on Data Science for Social Good, pp. 1-6.

Buchholz, K. (2020). Infographic: Where Climate Change Deniers Live, https://www.statista.com/chart/19449/countries-with-biggest-share-of-climate-change-deniers/.

Du, X., Emebo, O., Varde, A., Tandon, N., Chowdhury, S. N., and Weikum, G. (2016). Air quality assessment from social media and structured data: Pollutants and health impacts in urban planning, IEEE ICDE (International Conference on Data Engineering) workshops, pp. 54-59.

Gurajala, S., Dhaniyala, S., and Matthews, J. N. (2019). Understanding public response to air quality using tweet analysis, Social Media+ Society, 5(3), 2056305119867656.

Hutto, C., and Gilbert, E. (2014). Vader: A parsimonious rule-based model for sentiment analysis of social media text, AAAI conf. on web and social media, 8(1):216-225.

Iglesias, C. A., Sanchez-Rada, J. F., Vulcu, G., & Buitelaar, P. (2017). Linked Data Models for Sentiment and Emotion Analysis in Social Networks, Sentiment Analysis in Social Networks (pp. 49-69). Morgan Kaufmann.

Jiang, H., Lin, P., and Qiang, M. (2016). Public-opinion sentiment analysis for large hydro projects, Journal of Construction Engineering and Management, 142(2), 05015013.

McNamee B, Varde A. (2022), https://github.com/brad-mcnamee/climate-sentiment

Nickolas, S. (2021). What Do Correlation Coefficients Positive, Negative, and Zero Mean?. pp. 1-3. https://www.investopedia.com/ask/answers/032515/what-does-it-mean-if-correlation-coefficient-positive-negative-or-zero.asp

Puri, M., Dau, Z., Varde, A. (2021) COVID and social media: analysis of COVID-19 and social media trends for smart living and healthcare. ACM SIGWEB (Autumn): 5:1-5:20.

Razniewski, S., Tandon, N., and Varde, A. S. (2021), Information to wisdom: commonsense knowledge extraction and compilation, ACM International Conference on Web Search and Data Mining, WSDM, pp. 1143-1146.

Tandon, N., Varde, A. S., and de Melo, G. (2018), Commonsense knowledge in machine intelligence, ACM SIGMOD Record, 46(4): 49-52.

Wang, Y. D., Fu, X. K., Jiang, W., Wang, T., Tsou, M. H., and Ye, X. Y. (2017). Inferring urban air quality based on social media, Computers, Environment and Urban Systems, 66, 110-116.

Proceedings of the SALLD-2 Workshop @LREC2020, pages 31–38
Language Resources and Evaluation Conference (LREC 2022), Marseille, 24 June 2022

Sentiment Analysis of Sentences from Serbian ELTeC corpus

Ranka Stanković, Miloš Košprdić, Milica Ikonić Nešić, Tijana Radović
University of Belgrade, Serbia, Studenski Trg 1, Belgrade, Serbia
ranka.stankovic@rgf.bg.ac.rs, tijana.n.radovic@gmail.com,
milica.ikonic.nesic@fil.bg.ac.rs, milos.kosprdic@gmail.com

Abstract

In this paper we present first study of Sentiment Analysis (SA) of Serbian novels from the 1840-1920 period. The preparation of sentiment lexicon was based on three existing lexicons: *NRC*, *AFFIN* and *Bing* with additional extensive corrections. The first phase of dataset refinement included filtering the word that are not found in Serbian morphological dictionary and in second automatic POS tagging and lemma were manually corrected. The polarity lexicon was extracted and transformed into *ontolex-lemon* and published as initial version. The complex inflection system of Serbian language required expansion of sentiment lexicon with inflected forms from Serbian morphological dictionaries. Set of sentences for SA was extracted from 120 novels of Serbian part of ELTeC collection, labelled for polarity and used for several model training. Several approaches for SA are compared, starting with for variation of lexicon based and followed by Logistic Regression, Naive Bayes, Decision Tree, Random Forest, SVN and k-NN. The comparison with models trained on labelled movie reviews dataset indicates that it can not successfully be used for sentiment analysis of sentences in old novels.

Keywords: sentiment lexicon, sentiment analysis, distant-reading, machine learning, old novels

1. Introduction

This paper presents Sentiment Analysis (SA) on a corpus of Serbian novels, from the 1840 – 1920 period, that is being developed under the umbrella of the "Distant Reading for European Literary History" COST Action CA16204, using different methods, including lexicon based SA. The lexicon based approach of SA for Serbian is not much used due to the lack of sentiment lexicons for Serbian. We have decided to work on development of the Serbian Sentiment Lexicon which will contribute in overcoming this gap. This paper presents first results in this research, including publishing lexical resource as Linguistic Linked Open Data in order to provide and enable further research of SA on different corpora written in Serbian.

The inspiration was found in lexicons described in (Iglesias and Sánchez-Rada, 2021), especially on a polarity lexicon of Latin lemmas, called LatinAffectus which is a part of LiLa – Linked Data-based Knowledge Base of Linguistic Resources and NLP tool for Latin language (Sprugnoli et al., 2020). The objective of LiLa was to connect and ultimately exploit the wealth of linguistic resources and NLP tools for Latin created so far, in order to bridge the gap between raw language data, NLP and knowledge descriptions, so in line with that our objective is to expand and enrich tools for NLP in Serbian language by creating this lexicon. Sprugnoli et al. (Sprugnoli et al., 2021) introduced fourth category: *mixed* where the opposite emotions where produced and it is not possible to find a clearly prevailing emotion (between lexicon and evoked images). It could be seen that it is somehow similar to our category "both", but we did not go in this direction since there were so few those entries, so we just eliminated them.

Hybrid sentiment analysis framework for a morphologically rich language (SAFOS) (Mladenović et al., 2016) used a sentiment lexicon and Serbian WordNet (SWN) synsets assigned with sentiment polarity scores in the process of feature selection. They expanded the lexicon generated using SWN, by adding morphological forms of emotional terms and phrases using Serbian Morphological Electronic Dictionaries (Krstev, 2008). Testing was performed on news and movie reviews, the best classification accuracy scores were achieved for the combination of unigram and bigram features reduced by sentiment feature mapping (accuracy 78.3 % for movie reviews and 79.2 % for news test set).

The sentiment analysis on Serbian Movie Review Dataset achieved best accuracy 85.5% for 2 classes and 62.2% for 3 classes, by using unigram, bigram and trigram features in a combination of l Naïve Bayes (NB) and Support Vector Machines (SVM) (Batanović et al., 2016).

Improving sentiment analysis for twitter data by handling negation rules in the Serbian language (Ljajić and Marovac, 2019) was based on grammatical rules that influence the change of polarity are processed. A statistically significant relative improvement was obtained (up to 31.16% or up to 2.65%) when the negation was processed using rules with the lexicon-based approach or machine learning methods. By applying machine learning methods, an accuracy of 68.84% was achieved on a set of positive, negative and neutral tweets, and an accuracy of as much as 91.13% when applied to the set of positive and negative tweets.

The NgramSPD (Graovac et al., 2019) explored n-gram models in conjunction with k Nearest Neighbourhood (kNN), Support Vector Machine (SVM) and Maximum Entropy (MaxEnt) algorithms to determine opinion polarity of the seven publicly available movie review benchmarks in Arabic, Czech, English, French, Spanish, Turkish, and Serbian. Formal evaluation confirmed that the proposed byte and character n-gram models outperform word n-gram model, and in conjunction with the presented MaxEnt algorithm outperform other machine learning supervised techniques used with more complex document representation approaches. Despite their simplicity and broad applicability, byte and character n-grams have been shown to be able to capture information on different levels – lexical and syntactic. For *SerbMR-2* best performance was achieved with accuracy 85.54% by maxEnt, while with kNN 81.14% and SVM 83.47%.

2. Sentiment Lexicons

2.1. Existing Sentiment Lexicons

In the lexicon-based approach the polarity of the text is determined on the basis of a set of positive, negative and neutral words (Mostafa and Nebot, 2020). To implement a semantically based approach, lexicons of sentiments are used, in which words are classified as positive, negative or neutral according to its polarity. The polarity of the whole text represent a combination of the polarity of the words that make up the text. Currently, there is large number of different lexicons of sentiments however, three that are most commonly used (Silge and Robinson, 2017) are: *Bing* (Liu et al., 2004), *NRC* (Mohammad and Turney, 2010) i *AFINN* (Nielsen, 2011).

The *NRC* lexicon of Sentiments (Mohammad and Turney, 2010) classify words according to polarity as positive or negative, and according to the category of emotions to which they belong (anger, fear, anticipation, trust, surprise, sadness, joy, and disgust). Determining the polarity and the category of emotions to which words belong was manually done by crowd-sourcing. The *AFINN* lexicon is a list of English terms manually rated for valence with an integer between -5 (negative) and +5 (positive) (Nielsen, 2011). The *Bing* sentiment lexicon is a general purpose English sentiment lexicon that consists of manually categorized words in a binary fashion, either positive or negative (Liu et al., 2004).

These three lexicons can be found as a part of numerous packages that are used for lexicon-based sentiment analysis in R programming language such as *tidytext* described in (Silge and Robinson, 2017) and *syzhet* (Jockers and Thalken, 2020). The tidytext package (Silge and Robinson, 2017) specializes in preprocessing, analyzing, and visualizing textual data. Also, this package provides access to *NRC*, *AFINN* and *Bing* lexicons of sentiments which enables extraction of sentiments in text. Syuzhet package (Jockers and Thalken, 2020) comes with four sentiment dictionaries and provides a method for accessing the robust, but computationally expensive, sentiment extraction tool developed in the NLP group at Stanford. The main functions in the package are quickly extraction of sentiments from your own text files. More precisely, this package serves to extracts sentiment and sentiment-derived plot arcs from text using a variety of sentiment dictionaries conveniently packaged for consumption by R users. Implemented dictionaries include *syuzhet'* developed in the Nebraska Literary Lab, *Bing* (Liu et al., 2004), *NRC* (Mohammad and Turney, 2010) and *AFINN* (Nielsen, 2011). Althought, *Bing*, *NRC* and *AFINN* lexicon are widely use, there are sentiment analysis packages in R that use other sentiment lexicons.

The Sentiment Analysis package (Pröllochs et al., 2018) (Nicolas Proellochs and Stefan Feuerriege, 2021) introduces a powerful toolchain facilitating the sentiment analysis of textual contents in R. This implementation utilizes various existing dictionaries, such as QDAP (Qualitative Data Analysis Package) and, Harvard IV and Loughran-McDonald. Furthermore, it can also create customized dictionaries. The latter function uses LASSO regularization as a statistical approach to select relevant terms based on an exogenous response variable. Finally, all methods can be easily compared using built-in evaluation routines.

Lexicon of sentiments created for this research is based on three existing lexicons: *NRC*, *AFFIN* and *Bing* with additional extensive manual corrections.

2.2. Senti-Pol-sr Sentiment Lexicon

Entries from *NRC*, *AFFIN* and *Bing* lexicons are available in Serbian or Serbo-Croatian but mostly by automatic translation with numerous entries with translation errors and English terms instead of Serbian translation equivalent. The headwords of three lexicons were merged, duplicate entries were removed and union of polarities were assigned in the first step. The shallow lexicon was produced, where not all headwords were assigned all categories. However, polarity -1, 1 was either assigned or possible to derived for all. For AFINN lexicon from -5 to -2 was assigned -1 (negative), -1, 0, +1 were assigned 0 (neutral) and from +2 to +5 (positive).

Several entries in Serbian side of lexicon were multiple since different English words had same translation e.g. *odvratan* is aligned with *depraved, despicable, disgusting, distasteful, distracted, hideous, loathsome, obnoxious, odious, revolting, sickening*, so the new acquiring a new list of entries with distinct headwords in Serbian was produced.

The elimination of words that do not belong to Serbian language was based on Serbian morphological dictionaries (Krstev and Vitas, 2006) that are managed by Leximirka developing environment (Stanković et al., 2019). If headword was not found in lexical database either as lemmatized or inflected form, it was eliminated. If the headword was not found as lemmatized but it was found as inflected form, the lemma was corrected. The part of speech label was also assigned to the new lexical entry. All words that were not in lexicon were removed for this experiment. However, for further research additional exploration off excluded dataset is envisaged.

The preliminary inspection ed that words are mostly

foreign *Hawking, headdress, idleness*, so proper translation is required. The evaluation of a lexicon was done by two annotators who used English dictionary Morton Benson in order to manually evaluate our new lexicon. While manually evaluating one of the challenges was status of those terms that in English are represented with one word, but translated into Serbian have two words, for example, English word *scapegoat* is in Serbian translated as two words *žrtveno jagnje*, or *hearse* as *mrtvačka kola*. Moreover, the similar problem was when translation equivalent is a phrase in Serbian: *forsooth (ma nemojte mi reći)* or *halfway (na pola puta)*. Also, some adverbs and adjectives in English have the same form and they occurred in the lexicon twice but as different part of speech, for example the word *hilarious* was tagged as an adjective and as an adverb.
The manual disambiguation, correction, exclusion of contradictory (different) polarity of the same word followed. A number of new entries with lexical variants and synonyms of already existing entries was introduced.
The overview of positive, negative, both positive and negative is given, with a total column at the end of Table1. The graphical overview is given in Figure 1.
For further analysis words that had both polarities were excluded.

	pos	neg	both	total
NRC	2231	3243	81	5555
AFFIN	1293	878		2171
Merged	5889	10197	225	16311
Filtered	3387	5058	154	8599
Distinct	2678	3628	148	6454

Table 1: The sentiment lexicon entries statistics table.

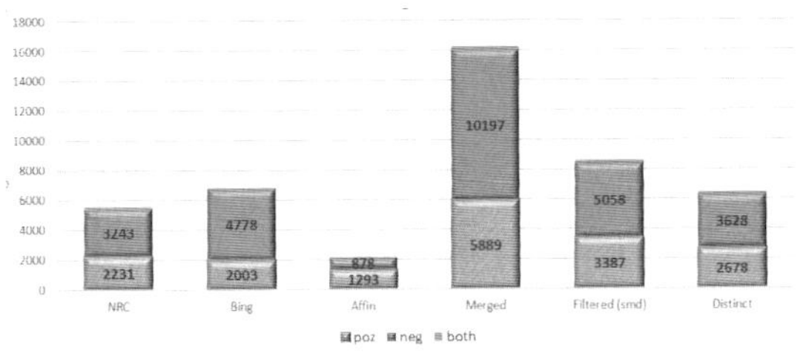

Figure 1: The sentiment lexicon entries statistics graph.

For transformation of produced lexicon *Senti-Pol-sr* into *ontolex-lemon* model (McCrae et al., 2011; McCrae et al., 2017) we adapted procedure in Leximir tool (Stanković and Krstev, 2012), based on approach described in (Ranka et al., 2018) and adapted . The initial form of lexicon (Stanković et al., 2022) is published in: http://llod.jerteh.rs/SA/. An excerpt of lexicon is:

```
:SentiPolLexicon a lime:Lexicon;
  dct:title "SentiPol"@sr;
  lime:entry :lex_folirant;
  lime:language "sr"^^xsd:language .

:lex_folirant a ontolex:LexicalEntry;
   ontolex:canonicalForm :form_folirant;
   rdfs:label "folirant"@sr;
   lexinfo:partOfSpeech "noun"@sr;
   ontolex:sense :sense1_folirant-n-0-sense1.

:form_folirant a ontolex:Form;
   ontolex:writtenRep "folirant"@sr.

:sense1_folirant marl:hasPolarity
   "hasPolarity:Negative";
   marl:hasValue "hasValue:-1".
```

Senti-Pol-sr ontolex-lemon version is loaded in Vocbench (Stellato et al., 2015) for further exploration and refinement and for retrieval via SPARQL endpoint. Figure 2 presents a list of enties starting with *s* focused on *sreća* (happiness) with positive polarity. (Armando Stellato et al., 2021)

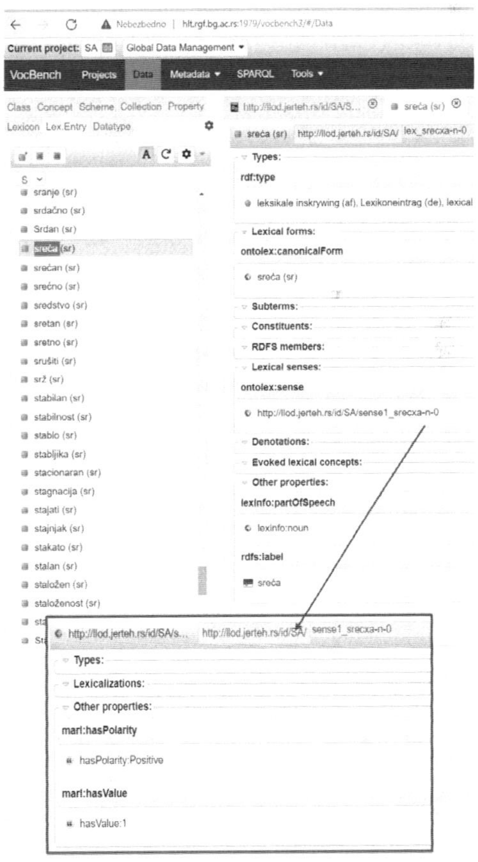

Figure 2: The sentiment lexicon in VocBench.

3. Labeled Dataset Preparation

3.1. Annotation guidelines

The annotations were done on a sentence level. The annotator's job was to determine is the given sentence positive, negative or neutral. In order to determine the polarity of the sentence annotator should rely on its intuition as a native speaker of a given language. The lack of these approach is that for some sentences such as sarcastic sentences or sentences when one side wins against another may be hard to determine the polarity of the sentence without given specifications about what is positive, what is negative and what is neutral (Mohammad, 2016).

In order to determine the polarity of sentence the annotator should consider positive all sentences that express support, admiration, positive attitude, forgiveness, fostering, success, positive emotional state. Negative sentences are those that include expressions of criticism, judgment, negative attitude, questioning validity/competence, failure, negative emotion. Finally, when the speaker is neither using positive language nor using negative language only giving the description of some event or place or talking about facts those sentences are marked as neutral (Mohammad, 2016).

While annotating, it was important that agreeing or disagreeing with the speaker's views should not have a bearing on annotator's response. The job of the annotator is to assess the language being used (not the views of the speaker). For example, the sentence, 'Evolution makes no sense', should be marked as negative since the speaker's words are criticizing or judging negatively something (in this case the theory of evolution). Note that the answer is not contingent on whether you believe in evolution or not. This approach groups the speaker's emotional state, speaker's opinion, and description of valanced events all into one category and aims simply to determine the dominant sentiment inferable from the sentence. For example, 'Yay! Novak beats Nadal 3–2' will be marked as positive because the speaker is using the positive expression 'Yay!'. Also, in the example 'Serbia lost to Montenegro' it may be difficult to annotate with respect to the opinion of the speaker towards the Serbian team, but the framing of the event as a loss is easily identified as negative expression (Mohammad, 2016).

3.2. Sentiment Dataset

The ELTeC[1] (Odebrecht et al., 2021) multilingual corpus of novels written in the time period 1840–1920 is built to test various distant reading methods among them sentiment analysis. Serbian part of ELTeC corpus (Krstev, 2021), dubbed *SrpELTeC*, comprises 100 novels in main collection and 20 in extended collection. The novels have structural annotations, sentence splitting, words are POS-tagged, lemmatized and seven classes of named entities are annotated (Stanković et al., 2022a).

From srpELTeC novels collection set of 30K sentences was extracted, relaying on sentence segmentation encoded in TEI XML, with <s> XMLS element. The <s> element was used to mark orthographic sentences, or any other segmentation of a text, provided that the segmentation is end-to-end, complete, and non-nesting. The number of positive and negative words was computed and assigned to each sentence. Sentences with different size and with different number of positive and negative words (according to lexicon presented in 2.2) were chosen. The set of sentences for manual evaluation was selected in several runs. The evaluation started with set where 5 or more positive words were found, than where 5 or more negative words was found. In second run set of sentences with at least one occurrences form sentiment lexicon was found and at the end without word from lexicon. The goal was to produce balances set with equal number of positive, neutral and negative sentences.

Four evaluators evaluated 1320 sentences and each sentence was evaluated by two evaluators. For 1089 evaluators had an agreement while 231 sentences were labeled differently. Inter-annotator agreement was calculated using ReCal2 tool (Deen Freelon, 2011) that show: Percent Agreement 82.5%, Scott's Pi 0.737, Cohen's Kappa 0.739, Krippendorff's Alpha (nominal) 0.737.

For this experiment we proceeded with sentences where evaluators had an agreement and the rest of the sentences will be later harmonised. At the end, in each class: positive, neutral and negative, there was 363 sentences. For 2 class classification only 726 senteces was used were data set is named *SrpELTeC-2C* and for 3 class classification 1089 named *SrpELTeC-3C*.

4. Sentiment Analysis

4.1. Experimental Approach

The sentiment data set from Section 3.2 with sentences from SrpELTeC novel collection in this section will be analysed by several models. In the first approach we analysed lexicon based model on both data sets *SrpELTeC-2C* and *SrpELTeC-3C* using different experiments with lexicon based models, including also combination of lexicon based models with other approaches witch will be describe briefly in Section 4.2.

In Section 4.3 will be given binary classification on *SerbMR-2C* and *SrpELTeC-2C* dataset using different methods for binary classification. By using Logistic Regression, Decision Tree, Random Forest and k-NN we trained models on datasets: *SerbMR-2C* (The Serbian movie review dataset, 2 classes) (Batanović et al., 2016) and on dataset *SrpELTeC-2C* (The Serbian ELTeC novels dataset, 2 classes). The models were evaluated and the results were compared . Logistic Regression and SVM using n-grams shown that results can be different quality using different n-grams vectoriza-

[1]ELTeC: European Literary Text Collection

tion. For the purpose of this research we compared trained models on *SerbMR-2C* dataset and evaluated on *SrpELTeC-2C* as vice verse. In further work is planed to do the same on data set with tree classes.

Classification of novel's sentences based on their sentiment show that the results on lexicon based approach are better than trained models. The outcome was expected, since in case of SerbMR-2C, the dataset used for training was on movies review and lexica and language style are different than in old novels, while for *SrpELTeC-2C* the dataset was too small.

4.2. Lexicon Based Classification

In this section we present different lexicon based models approaches using our produced lexicon on the *SrpELTeC-3C* dataset, and we give the brief comparison with the same models on the *SrpELTeC-2C* dataset. For the purpose of this work we done few experiments inspired by solution published in (Mitrović, 2021):

- **Experiment 1**: Solution based only on the sentiment lexicon. The model is comprised of one parameter only - limit. The average polarity of each sentence (sample) is calculated (essentially whether there are more positive or negative words). The prediction takes into consideration the calculated average only if it is grater than the limit or not. For the three class data, the model is comprised of two parameters, the positive and the negative limit. The parameters determine whether the sentence is positive (if the mean word polarity is grater than positive limit), negative (if the mean word polarity is less than negative limit) or neutral (if the mean word polarity is between those limits).

- **Experiment 2**: Solution based only on the sentiment lexicon, however this time it takes into consideration the ratio of positive / negative and the total number of words in the sentence.

- **Experiment 3**: Baseline model using Multinomial Naïve Bayes (MNB) with features only devised from the sentiment lexicon.

- **Experiment 4**: Baseline model using MNB with Bag-of-Words approach combined with the features of the sentiment lexicon.

Table 2 represent accuracy for four lexicon based experiments explained above with comparison on two evaluation datasets. The results that are much worse on SrpELTeC data are probably caused by lexical variety in novels and the fact that the novels might have lexica that is not in common used nowadays.

The best results were achieved in Experiment 4 and confusion matrix for two classes is presented in Figure 3 and Figure 4.

Accuracy	SerbMR–2C	SrpELTeC–3C
Experiment 1	0.864	0.649
Experiment 2	0.849	0.576
Experiment 3	0.848	0.657
Experiment 4	**0.878**	**0.719**

Table 2: Accuracy of SA on evaluation dataset for lexicon based experiments

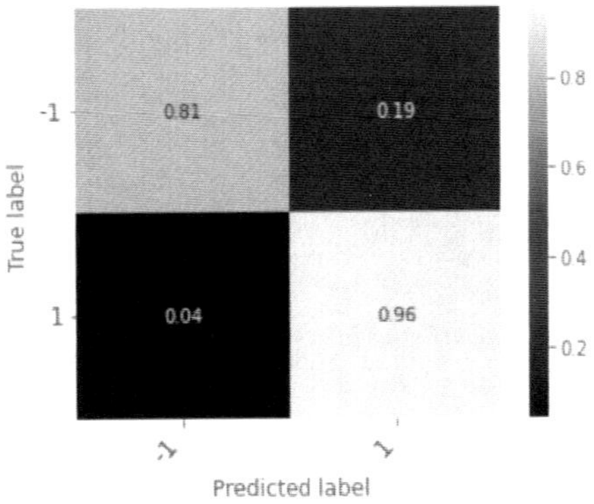

Figure 3: Confusion matrix for Experiment 4 with SrpELTeC-2C

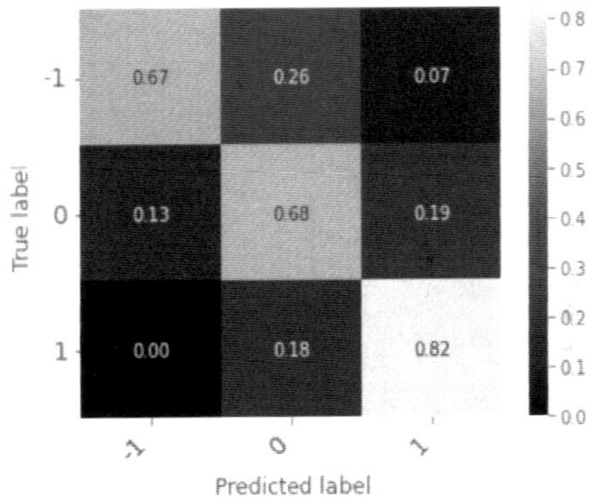

Figure 4: Confusion matrix for Experiment 4 with SrpELTeC-3C

4.3. Binary Classification on *SerbMR-2C* and *SrpELTeC-2C* dataset

In this section, we will approach the task of analyzing sentiments as a task of binary classification. We will get acquainted with three algorithms for classifying classical machine learning: logistic regression, random forests and k-nearest neighbors, and at the end, we will compare the performance of the model on two data sets *SerbMR-2C* and *SrpELTeC-2C* dataset.

The first machine learning algorithm we will encounter is logistic regression, as one of the basic algorithms of binary classification, so it is often encountered in comparative analyzes of model performance as a base model. The following Figure 5 shows the vocabulary words most deserving of the classification of texts by sentiment.

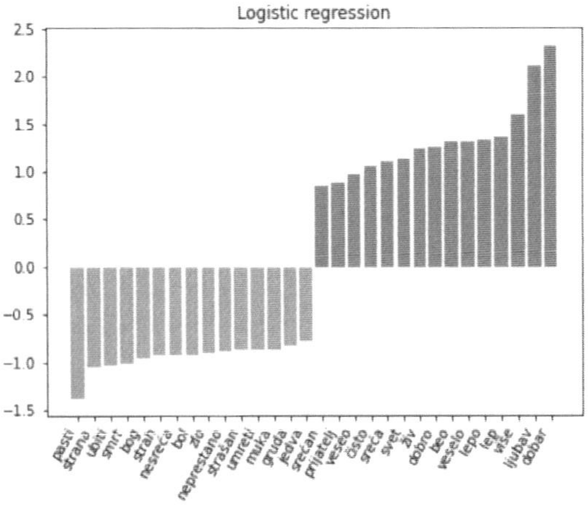

Figure 5: The vocabulary words.

The second algorithm was a decision tree, as an algorithm that learn a set of rules that can determine whether an instance is positive or negative. The Figure 6 presents the tree where in each node of the tree, the test is stated, then the value of the homogeneity measure used, the total number of instances analyzed, as well as the number of instances by classes.

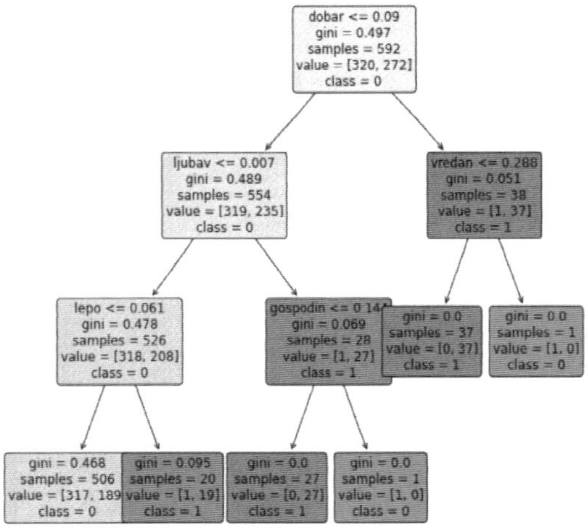

Figure 6: The decision tree subset.

For the next type of training we used Random Forest and k-nearest neighbors (KNN) algorithm for k = 3. The Table 3 presents accuracy for 4 methods on two datasets: trained on 80%, tested 10% and evaluated on 10% of the same dataset. For each dataset, the training model performance is evaluated for original and lemmatized text and the best accuracy for each dataset is emphasized. The part of speech tagging and lemmatization was performed using tagger for Serbian (Stanković et al., 2022b) that is using (Krstev et al., 2021; Škorić and Stanković, 2021). Results clearly show that lemmatized option achieve better accuracy.

Method	SerbMR-2C		SrpELTeC-2C	
accuracy	token	lemma	token	lemma
Log. Regr.	0.828	**0.831**	0.768	**0.878**
Dec. Tree	0.590	0.597	0.561	0.621
Rand. for.	0.692	0.733	0.698	0.681
k-NN	0.656	0.674	0.657	0.757

Table 3: Evaluation of four SA models on *SerbMR-2C* and SrpELTeC-2C

Logistic Regression gave the best accuracy (Table 3), so in addition to previously evaluated model using tf–idf representation, we proceeded with further training on unigrams, bigrams and trigrams using lemmatized *SrpELTeC-2C* text. However, we included also SVM in this phase and the results are presented in Table 4.

Model accuracy	Log. Reg.	SVM
tf-idf vec.	**0.878**	**0.891**
unigram vec.	0.877	0.876
bigram vec.	0.592	0.601
trigram vec.	0.521	0.531

Table 4: SrpELTeC accuracy of SA on evaluation dataset for Logistic Regression and SVM

The research question was: can we use model trained on one dataset for SA of another? Namely, can *SerbMR-2C* (more that double in size in number of samples, but much more in number of words) be used for *SrpELTeC-2C* SA (and vice versa)?
Two experiments were conducted using different datasets for training and evaluation:

- **Experiment 5**: Trained model on *SrpELTeC-2C* dataset and evaluated on 10% of *SerbMR-2C* dataset (169 reviews)
- **Experiment 6**: Trained model on *SerbMR-2C* dataset and evaluated on 10% of *SrpELTeC-2C* dataset (66 sentences)

Table 5 shows that the accuracy is much lower that those presented in Table 3 and Table 4. We suspect that the reason is the difference in lexica and language style between the datasets *SerbMR-2C* and SrpELTeC-2C. So we conclude that in order to achieve better performance we have to proceed with enlarging SrpELTeC dataset for model training.

Model accuracy	Experiment 5	Experiment 6
Log. Reg.	0.550	**0.681**
Dec. Tree	**0.556**	0.454
Random forest	**0.556**	0.575
k-NN	0.474	0.467

Table 5: Accuracy of SA on cross-dataset evaluation

5. Conclusion

We outlined the research on development and application of sentiment lexicon, (sentence) dataset labelling and training of the models for sentiment analysis. The challenges in these tasks were discussed, as well as statistics of developed resources and performance of the training models. The first presented approach was with lexicon based model using four different experiments, with the best accuracy 87.8% on the *SrpELTeC-2C* and 71.9% on the *SrpELTeC-3C* using MNB with Bag-of-Words approach combined with the features of our sentiment lexicon (experiment 4). The second approach was based on trained models Logistic Regression, Decision Tree, Random Forest and k-NN using labeled datasets. The Logistic Regression gave the best accuracy 87.8%. By preliminary comparison of miss-classified sentences we have fond missing entries in a lexicon: *zavoleti (fall in love)*, *milina (grace, enjoyment)*, *nesrećnik (unfortunate person)*, *sirotinja (poor people)* etc. The current activities are focused on producing larger set of manually evaluated sentences that will enable more suitable training dataset. The analysis of miss-classified sentences with lexicon-based approach will be used for lexicon improvement. Final version of lexicon will be published also in ELG portal (Rehm et al., 2020) and in a public SPARQL endpoint. Plan is also to add examples to the lexicon using FrAC - frequency and attestations for *ontolex-lemon* (Chiarcos et al., 2020). First steps towards RDF editions of the ELTeC corpus are publishing two Serbian novels Ivkova slava : pripovetka (Ivko's patron saint's day: a short story) and Nečista Krv (Impure blood), POS-tagged, lemmatized, with NER and NEL with Wikidata, available in NIF (Ikonić Nešić and Stanković, 2022), so integration and futher conversion is envisaged.

Further research will be guided towards 1) fine-tuning the lexicon: adding synonyms and antonyms, adding words found in positive and negative sentences that were "missed" by dictionary approach 2) including word embeddings in model training, 3) analyse sentences with negation in context that is related to sentiment.

6. Acknowledgements

The presented work is supported by the the COST Action CA18209 – NexusLinguarum "European network for Web-centred linguistic data science" and the COST Action 16204 – Distant Reading for European Literary History support. The authors would like to thank Mihailo Škorić for lemmatization, and Biljana Rujević for participation in the sentiment annotation.

7. Bibliographical References

Batanović, V., Nikolić, B., and Milosavljević, M. (2016). Reliable baselines for sentiment analysis in resource-limited languages: The serbian movie review dataset. In *in Proceedings of the 10th International Conference on Language Resources and Evaluation (LREC 2016)*, pages 2688–2696, Portorož, Slovenia.

Chiarcos, C., Ionov, M., de Does, J., Depuydt, K., Khan, F., Stolk, S., Declerck, T., and McCrae, J. P. (2020). Modelling frequency and attestations for ontolex-lemon. In *Proceedings of the 2020 Globalex Workshop on Linked Lexicography*, pages 1–9.

Graovac, J., Mladenović, M., and Tanasijević, I. (2019). Ngramspd: Exploring optimal n-gram model for sentiment polarity detection in different languages. *Intelligent Data Analysis*, 23(2):279–296.

Iglesias, C. Á. and Sánchez-Rada, J. F. (2021). Sentiment analysis meets linguistic linked data: An overview of the state of the art. In *Workshop on Sentiment Analysis & Linguistic Linked Data, September 01, 2021, Zaragoza, Spain.*

Jockers, M. L. and Thalken, R. (2020). Sentiment analysis. In *Text Analysis with R*, pages 159–174. Springer.

Krstev, C. (2008). *Processing of Serbian. Automata, Texts and Electronic Dictionaries*. Faculty of Philology of the University of Belgrade.

Krstev, C. (2021). The serbian part of the eltec collection through the magnifying glass of metadata. *Infotheca - Journal for Digital Humanities*, 21(2):26–42.

Liu, B., Li, X., Lee, W. S., and Yu, P. S. (2004). Text classification by labeling words. In *Aaai*, volume 4, pages 425–430.

Ljajić, A. and Marovac, U. (2019). Improving sentiment analysis for twitter data by handling negation rules in the serbian language. *Computer Science and Information Systems*, 16(1):289–311.

McCrae, J., Spohr, D., and Cimiano, P., (2011). *Linking Lexical Resources and Ontologies on the Semantic Web with Lemon*, pages 245–259. Springer Berlin Heidelberg, Berlin, Heidelberg.

McCrae, J. P., Bosque-Gil, J., Gracia, J., Buitelaar, P., and Cimiano, P. (2017). The ontolex-lemon model: development and applications. In *Proceedings of eLex 2017 conference*, pages 19–21.

Mladenović, M., Mitrović, J., Krstev, C., and Vitas, D. (2016). Hybrid sentiment analysis framework for a morphologically rich language. *Journal of Intelligent Information Systems*, 46(3):599–620.

Mohammad, S. and Turney, P. (2010). Emotions evoked by common words and phrases: Using mechanical turk to create an emotion lexicon. In *Proceedings of the NAACL HLT 2010 workshop on computational approaches to analysis and generation of emotion in text*, pages 26–34.

Mohammad, S. (2016). A practical guide to sentiment annotation: Challenges and solutions. In *Proceedings of the 7th workshop on computational approaches to subjectivity, sentiment and social media analysis*, pages 174–179.

Mostafa, M. M. and Nebot, N. R. (2020). The arab image in spanish social media: A twitter sentiment analytics approach. *Journal of Intercultural Communication Research*, 49(2):133–155.

Nielsen, F. Å. (2011). A new anew: Evaluation of a word list for sentiment analysis in microblogs. *arXiv preprint arXiv:1103.2903*.

Pröllochs, N., Feuerriegel, S., and Neumann, D. (2018). Statistical inferences for polarity identification in natural language. *PloS one*, 13(12):e0209323.

Ranka, S., Cvetana, K., Biljana, L., and Mihailo, Š. (2018). Electronic dictionaries-from file system to lemon based lexical database. In *Proceedings of the 11th International Conference on Language Resources and Evaluation-W23 6th Workshop on Linked Data in Linguistics: Towards Linguistic Data Science (LDL-2018), LREC 2018, Miyazaki, Japan, May 7-12, 2018*, pages 48–56.

Rehm, G., Berger, M., Elsholz, E., Hegele, S., and et al., F. K. (2020). European language grid: An overview. *CoRR*, abs/2003.13551.

Silge, J. and Robinson, D. (2017). *Text mining with R: A tidy approach.* " O'Reilly Media, Inc.".

Sprugnoli, R., Mambrini, F., Moretti, G., and Passarotti, M. (2020). Towards the modeling of polarity in a latin knowledge base. In *WHiSe@ ESWC*, pages 59–70.

Sprugnoli, R., Mambrini, F., Passarotti, M., and Moretti, G. (2021). Sentiment analysis of latin poetry: First experiments on the odes of horace. In *Proceedings of the Eighth Italian Conference on Computational Linguistics (CLiC-it 2021). Milan, Italy, January 26-28, 2022*, pages 1–7. CEUR Workshop Proceedings (CEUR-WS. org).

Stanković, R., Krstev, C., Šandrih Todorović, B., and Škorić, M. (2022a). Annotation of the serbian eltec collection. *Infotheca - Journal for Digital Humanities*, 21(2):43–59.

Stanković, R., Škorić, M., and Šandrih Todorović, B. (2022b). Parallel bidirectionally pretrained taggers as feature generators. *Applied Sciences*, 12(10).

Stellato, A., Rajbhandari, S., Turbati, A., Fiorelli, M., Caracciolo, C., Lorenzetti, T., Keizer, J., and Pazienza, M. T. (2015). Vocbench: A web application for collaborative development of multilingual thesauri. In Fabien Gandon, et al., editors, *The Semantic Web. Latest Advances and New Domains*, pages 38–53, Cham. Springer International Publishing.

8. Language Resource References

Armando Stellato et al. (2021). *VocBench*. University of Rome Tor Vergata, Italy, `http://vocbench.uniroma2.it/`, 3.0.

Deen Freelon. (2011). *Reliability Calculator for 2 coders*. Deen Freelon, `http://dfreelon.org/utils/recalfront/recal2/#doc`, 1.0.

Milica Ikonić Nešić and Ranka Stanković. (2022). *srpNIF*. `http://llod.jerteh.rs/ELTEC/srp/NIF/`.

Cvetana Krstev and Duško Vitas. (2006). *SrpMD - Serbian morphological dictionaries*. ELG, `https://live.european-language-grid.eu/catalogue/lcr/17355`, 1.0.

Cvetana Krstev and Duško Vitas and Ranka Stanković and Mihailo Škorić. (2021). *SrpMD4Tagging - Serbian Morphological Dictionaries for Tagging*. ELG, `https://live.european-language-grid.eu/catalogue/lcr/9294`, 1.0.

Miljan Mitrović. (2021). *Sentiment Analysis SerbMR*. github.

Nicolas Proellochs and Stefan Feuerriege. (2021). *R Package 'SentimentAnalysis': Dictionary-Based Sentiment Analysis*. github, `https://github.com/sfeuerriegel/SentimentAnalysis`, 1.3-4.

Carolin Odebrecht and Lou Burnard and Christof Schöch. (2021). *European Literary Text Collection (ELTeC): April 2021 release with 14 collections of at least 50 novels*. Zenodo, `https://github.com/COST-ELTeC`.

Ranka Stanković and Cvetana Krstev. (2012). *LeXimir - Tool for lexical resources management and query expansion*. 1.0.

Ranka Stanković and Cvetana Krstev and Mihailo Škorić and Biljana Lazić. (2019). *Leximirka - lexicographic database and a web application for developing, managing and exploring lexicographic data*. 1.0.

Ranka Stanković and Tijana Radović and Miloš Kosprdić. (2022). *Senti-Pol-sr - Lexicon for sentiment analisys, draft version*. 1.0.

Mihailo Škorić and Ranka Stanković. (2021). *SrpKor4Tagging-TreeTagger*. ELG, `https://live.european-language-grid.eu/catalogue/ld/9296`, 1.0.

Author Index